D1647368

WILLIAM MACGILLIVRAY

A Walk To London

Edited by Dr Robert Ralph

acair

Acair acknowledges the permission of The University of Aberdeen
to publish this journal and the financial collaboration in bringing
this project to fruition.

Acair is also grateful for assistance from the following persons
who provided financial sponsorship:
Mr Jonathan Bulmer, The North Harris Estate
Dr David Horrobin
Ms Tessa Tennant
Mr A. M. Pelham Burn

Acair thanks Dr Robert Ralph who edited the journal and provided
advice and guidance throughout the preparatory process.

First published in Scotland in 1998 by Acair Ltd., 7 James Street
Stornoway, Isle of Lewis.

Cover and book designed at Acair by Margaret Anne Macleod
Printed by ColourBooks Ltd., Dublin

ISBN 0 86152 173 0 (Paperback)
ISBN 0 86152 174 9 (Hardback)

Contents

Foreword

William MacGillivray was 23 years old when he decided to walk from Aberdeen to London. His purpose was to visit the British Museum to see the natural history collections there, especially the collection of birds.

MacGillivray was born in Old Aberdeen in 1796, the illegitimate son of a student at the local university, Kings College. His father, also William, came from Harris and soon after his son's birth, he joined the Cameron Highlanders and served in the Peninsular Wars, where he was killed. The young William MacGillivray, at the age of three, was taken to Harris and brought up on his uncle's farm at Northton. He developed an interest in all aspects of natural history, in geology, botany, and zoology, an interest that was increased by what he saw on the long walks between Harris and university in Aberdeen at beginnings and ends of the academic year. He took an MA degree and began to study medicine but never completed his degree in the subject. In the summer of 1817 he returned to the Western Isles where he spent a year in and around Northton. He kept a detailed journal that describes the events of the year, observations of his daily life, the weather, the people that he met, the clothes that he wore, and records of the plants and animals that he saw. In the journal he also reflected on his plans for the future and his growing ambition to become an ornithologist.

His visit to London, to the British Museum, was one of the first steps towards realising that ambition. From Aberdeen to London by the most direct route is about 500 miles but MacGillivray took a circuitous path and had walked 501 miles before he crossed the border into England at Carlisle. He took a roundabout route through Scotland to see parts of the country that he had not visited before, to increase his general knowledge of its natural history, especially its botany. Almost every evening he wrote up his journal describing the events of the day, finishing with a list of the plants and animals that he had seen, sometimes working by candlelight long into the night. After crossing the border his natural history records are less detailed but he continued to write about the places that he went through and the people that he met. He arrived in London having walked 828 miles in eight weeks.

MacGillivray never wrote an autobiography but he wrote a number of journals and diaries, most of which were destroyed in a library fire in Australia at the end of the last century. Two have survived and are now in the care of the Special Collections Department of Aberdeen University Library. They were donated to the library in 1934 by Mr William Lachlan MacGillivray of Eoligary House in Barra, a nephew of William MacGillivray. The first of these journals, describing his year at Northton, was published by Acair Ltd in1996, *William MacGillivray - A Hebridean Naturalist's Journal 1817-1819*. This is the second journal, the record of his walk to London, a walk that confirmed his ambition to become an ornithologist.

Editorial Note

I became the curator of the Zoology Department Museum at Aberdeen University in 1990. Soon after taking on the position I realised that museum had been established by William MacGillivray when he was the Regius Professor of Natural History in the 1840s. My interest in him grew as I became aware of his many talents, his stature as a natural historian and as an ornithologist. I also became aware that he was almost unknown in his native land, when he should be recognised as Scotland's finest naturalist. In collecting material for a biography, published as *William MacGillivray* by HMSO in 1993, I realised that the Special Collections Department of the Aberdeen University Library held two of MacGillivray's original journals. This is the second to be published.

The journal as it is printed here is substantially as MacGillivray wrote it. I have retained his punctuation, use of capitals and spelling of place names. As in his Northton journal MacGillivray kept long lists of the animals and plants that he saw. He recorded them using their scientific Latin names. To make these lists in the journal more accessible I have added the English names and have removed the longer lists of specimens to an Appendix. At places in the journal MacGillivray refers to 'examining' or 'describing' a specimen. Used in this sense the words mean making a detailed comparison of a specimen with the published description, done in Latin, for example, the number of petals, sepals and other anatomical features.

MacGillivray wrote his journal with a quill pen and ink during an eight-week, 838-mile walk, sometimes by candlelight in a cold room, sometimes with frozen fingers while sheltering under a hedge and wondering where his next meal was coming from. Editing the manuscript on disk and screen has been done in considerably more comfort.

I am grateful to Principal C Duncan Rice for his interest in MacGillivray and for his encouragement in producing this book. I have to acknowledge the permission of the Aberdeen University Librarian to publish the journal and the staff of Acair for their help, enthusiasm and patience. I also have to thank the University of Aberdeen for the financial assistance that helped in the publication of the journal.

Dr Robert Ralph
Zoology Department
Aberdeen

January 1998

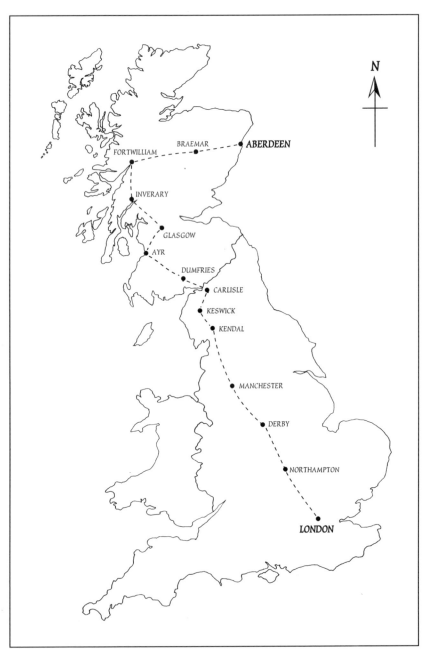

The route William MacGillivray took from Aberdeen to London.

Notes taken

in the course of a journey

from Aberdeen to London by Braemar,

Fort William, Inverary, Glasgow, Ayr, Dumfries,

Carlisle, Keswick, Kendal, Manchester,

Derby and Northampton,

in 1819

by

William MacGillivray.

Old Aberdeen, Tuesday 7th September, 1819.

I am at length free - yet not independent. Independence in the strictest sense of the term is not compatible with any modification of human nature - nor is freedom. But in a limited sense independence, for aught that I know to the contrary, may be attained by almost every person who has the free uses of his mental and corporeal organs, and of course by me. Yet, as I have said, I am not independent, and for the present must content me with exclaiming as I have already done "O thou noble spirit of Independence! When shall I again possess thee?" As to freedom, I have just got as much of it as I need at present - that is I am inclined to think so. I feel that I can either keep my seat or leave it - and being naturally, or perhaps from habit of a restless disposition I feel inclined even to bestir me and to be doing. In London city there is, I am told, a great collection of Beasts and Fishes, of Birds and other flying things, of Reptiles and Insects - in short of all the creatures which have been found upon the face of the earth. I hither therefore shall direct my steps - because I am desirous of furthering my cognition of these things. There is also a land in the isle in which mountain is heaped upon mountain, and which abounds in lakes and rivers and cascades in precipices, and caverns and vallies, and forests - but my enthusiasm has fallen asleep and I cannot rouse it, and without it how could I describe this land of the west to which I shall proceed without delay. Truly good cause have I to be ashamed of my inability to speak or to write - but ere six days be over the cause shall have vanished, and I shall once more be what I was when with wearied feet but lightsome spirit I traversed the sandy plains of Uist, or wandered among the rocks of Barray. Of late I have been plunged into the fearful gulph of actual existence - but my spirit shall soon rise from it to mingle with the great soul of the universe. Soon shall I again exclaim Majestic Nature! thou canst satisfy my every wish. Oh! with thee let me live and die. Thy beauties can never fade, nor can they ever cease to charm. But alas! there is a fearful void in my heart. I know not what I have become of late - there is a feeling of something wanting in my soul. Man is assuredly a social animal, and I am assuredly formed for a very impetuous excretion of affection toward one or more objects. This I thought I had indulged, but I now feel that there is not a soul upon earth with which I can hold free communion. Rather I have not yet found one, and till I find some dear - pah ! - there is a capriciousness in my nature which I combat in vain. Objects present themselves every day which I deem lovely, but no sooner have I examined them than by some accursed fatality they appear trivial or trifling. Yet full often does the tremor of sympathy gladden my heart, but it endures only for a moment. It is not in my heart or affections alone that this void exists - but also, as I have said in my mental frame - rather there is a wild and incomprehensible vortex which jumbles every perception, sensation and idea, producing the sense of nonentity in the midst of existence. This is the consequence of my disdain of all controls. I have taken upon me to think for myself, and ratiocination exerted without judgement or order has led me to reject all creeds and doctrines of faith, as the mere produce of human ingenuity. The rejection of a favourite object of whatever kind, even when we are convinced of its falsity is not easily performed. The heart must bleed when torn from the object to which it clings. Hence no man, who is not viciously inclined, can ever renounce the Christian religion, without experiencing a bitter pang. These pangs have now ceased in my breast, but an incomprehensible confusion of ideas has succeeded. This too will in time disappear. At present however there is scarcely a single object in moral existence of which I have definite ideas. Of one thing only I feel assured - the existence of a Deity. This in my estimation should be made the basis of all philosophy. Years upon years will have rolled their shadowy forms into the gulf of nonentity before serenity can visit my mind. Goethe says that man is never happy but either before he has attained his reason, or after he has lost it. This is not true. Without reason or the faculty of reflection there cannot be happiness. The pleasure of mere sensitive existence is not happiness. I have hinted my intention of undertaking a journey and to this topic I return from my digression. "The use of travelling" says Dr Johnson, is to regulate imagination by reality, and instead of thinking how things may be, to see them as they are. But with due deference to the Doctor, that is with no deference at all, for I disdain the controls of authority, I must indulge the inclination which I feel of criticising this opinion, and in the first place I shall use the phrase of Sterne, and say 'this I deny'. Such indeed might have been the principal use of travelling to Dr Johnson, whose sphere of observation was extremely limited, and whose imagination was therefore set in action to supply the deficiency. To such an animal the chief use of travelling is just such as has been stated. The error which he committed is a very common one; that of converting a particular remark into a general one. The uses of travelling are many nor is any one of them so pre-eminent as to justify attention to it solely. Some of these uses will occur to every one who thinks on the subject. But in truth the use ascribed by Dr Johnson is among the most uncommon, being applicable only to men of strong imaginations and little knowledge (if such a combination can exist) who are much better versed in creating new worlds than in comprehending those already formed, or to those pretty fellows who exhaust worlds and then imagine new - a fine idea of Mr Garrick's indeed! and perfectly suited to the very exquisite taste of those creatures who never penetrate an inch deep below the surface of a thing. Unfortunately for the expression however this same world of ours has never yet been quite exhausted, and I am somewhat apprehensive will not be these twenty years at least. So the idea must assuredly be esteemed bombastic. I have for some time entertained an idea that vanity has a much more extensive influence than is commonly supposed, and I believe many actions which are ascribed to widely different motives may be very easily be traced to it. Few, in truth, in my estimation, own a higher principle, and I believe that over myself it has had almost unlimited control for many years. The motives for this present journey are numerous. I have no peace of mind. Travelling invariably restores it in some degree. I wish to extend my knowledge in Natural History, especially in ornithology and botany. This can only be done by travelling. I wish to think at liberty, to scrutinise my own mind. Diversity of situation and circumstance is most favourable to this. I am tired of the dull reality of common life and am passionately fond of adventures. To the mountains of Albyn then, let me see human nature, let me study nature in general, let me make the best of my situation, let me steal away from myself as I am, and be for a short time what I would be always. I have been thinking of a general plan for my journal but have scarcely determined it. However I believe the following points are settled. I shall write it with as much freedom as if I were convinced that no person should ever read it. At the same time it must be so written that others may readily understand it upon perusal, that is, I must avoid obscurity, and instead of making it a mere collocation of memoranda must endeavour to write it with as much perspicuity as if I intended it for public inspection. A true and faithful account of the adventures, follies and blunders of any individual who is in any respect worthy of notice cannot fail to prove beneficial to others in many points. This utility therefore furnishes one motive for allowing several people to read my narrative, and a conviction that my sentiments will jar with those of most of its readers cannot deter me from giving it some degree of publicity; for I despise opinion unsupported by reason, detest bigotry, and rejoice in persecution, that is in being persecuted, but not in exercising any authority, much less persecution, over others. But while I write with the intention of benefitting others, and of gratifying my own vanity, I also write from the conviction that my notes will be useful to myself on many future occasions, yea even unto the day of my death. The idea of unity of design cannot then be carried through this narrative, and pieces intended for myself alone will necessarily be found mingled with those destined for the perusal of others. My determination of allowing several to read this journal is perfectly consonant with reason, at least perfectly natural, for man, as I have said is a social animal, social in his pleasures, in his misfortunes, and I would be acting from very selfish motives if I could write two quires of large paper merely for the sake of benefiting my own precious self. Every action or thought which is more or less proper or virtuous is always accompanied with numerous advantages, and although I have no inclination to adhere to virtue merely on account of its temporal rewards as divines call them, I may enumerate a few of the advantages likely to result from this supposed good action, or rather good intention, though in sooth it may be neither the one nor the other. This enumeration however I warn both my readers and myself will not be systematic. Improvement in style is dependent upon vanity because being anxious to appear to the best advantage, and knowing that my readers will all be more or less polished, I shall in common take great care to acquit myself as well as circumstances will permit. Extension of personal cognition, which is very desirable for many evident reasons. Mental improvement of two kinds, literary and moral, more especially the latter, and both dependent in a great measure upon vanity - for it is not desirable to appear less than one might be. These two departments branch out into an infinitude. Partly from the instigation of vanity, and partly from other motives, I refrain from laying down any general or particular plan either for my journey or journal. Only I shall drink a mouthful from the source of the Dee, and give three cheers to myself on the top of Ben Nevis; and till that time keep a regular list of all the plants and birds which may occur. On my back I carry a knapsack eighteen inches by fourteen, and three and a half in depth, made of very thick oiled cloth, and fastening with two leather straps. This machine which cost me six shillings and sixpence contains the following articles; a large portfolio containing a quire of large fine paper folded and marked at the margin for my journal, and seventeen pieces of drawing paper of the same size with the former. Two travelling maps, one of Scotland, the other of England, a small portfolio with a parcel of paper for drying plants, a few sheets of clean paper, stitched, Compendium Flora Britannica, a bottle of ink, four quills, China ink, paints, two black lead pencils, eight camel hair pencils with stalks, Indian rubber, a shirt, a false neck, two pairs of short stockings, a soap box, two razors, a piece of soap, a toothbrush, a sharping stone, a lancet, a pair of scissors, some thread, needles. My clothes are, an oldish hat, a flannel undervest, linen shirt of course, a blue long coat, gray trowsers, and black vest, the three last old materials, a pair of short stockings, a pair of stout shoes and a coloured neck cloth. Other articles will be mentioned tomorrow, after I have set out.

Charlestown of Aboyne, Wednesday 8th Sept. 8pm.

I rose today about half past four, breakfasted about five, and soon after set out. After passing through King Street, Castle Street, and the Shiprow, I got to Dee Side near Black's Brewery. Here I fixed my knapsack to my shoulders. The articles contained by it and by my pockets not mentioned are: a penknife, a small ink piece with pens, a small itinerary of Scotland, a glass for drinking by the way, a towel. To my dress or clothing I have added a greatcoat, and a pair of old gloves. Of money I had just Ten Pounds Sterling when I left Aberdeen; nine pounds in bank notes put into a small pocket in the inner side of my flannel undervest, one in silver, secured in a purse of chamois leather, kept in a pocket of my trowsers. I walked along the edge of the river until I came to the bridge by which I crossed it, and by doing so entered Kincardine or Mearns-Shire. The bridge consists of seven arches all equal in magnitude. This form is said to be particularly beautiful, I own it is so. A little above the bridge I asked of a milkmaid if the tide came up so far. "Aye" replied she 'fan't's griet, bit nae jish freely". Some miles further on the following questions were proposed to me by a country man "Di ye ken gien the Skule-maister o Nether Banchory be at home?" "Is't bukes at y'ere gaen about wi?" To both which I answered in the negative. Along this road which passes near the river the scenery is rather dullish for some miles, because the view is very limited. About five miles from town it improves greatly, there being a good view of the distant mountains, rising behind each other to a considerable height. Keeping upon the road I passed through the parishes of Banchory Devenack, Mary-culter, Durris, and about eighteen miles from town recrossed the Dee by a wooden bridge and entered Banchory Ternan. Hitherto the scenery has been uninteresting, but at Banchory there is a fine hollow inclosed by hills of considerable magnitude and well wooded. The natural wood along the river was also here greatly increased and the whole valley presented the appearance of a fine piece of land in the immediate neighbourhood of a great city, being thinly covered with houses, some of them gentees, according to the common phrase, although none of them are splendid. Here I drank a bottle of porter, about one o'clock. The cause of my detention by the road will appear in due time. Near the Bridge of Banchory on the south side of the Dee is a considerable stream which forms a fall, (the Falls of Feugh) in which was suspended a net made of wattles for the purpose of taking the fish as they were endeavouring to leap. As I was looking at this fall an old man came up and asked if I saw fish. He told me it is called the Water of Straen or Straar. Our very precious conversation terminated with his asking "Di ye get a hankle a thae bukes sane na?" and my answering that I did not. Such of the people of Banchory as I have heard speaking appear to have a slight, almost imperceptible degree of the South-country tone, as it is called at Aberdeen, awa. For five miles above Banchory the scenery is tolerable but for some miles farther up the river sterility predominates. About the twenty-third mile stone I left the road, cast off my coat, shoes and stockings and washed my feet and hands in the river. About a mile and a half farther on I passed the 'Brig o Pitargh' as a boy called it. The Bridge of Potarch consisting of three arches. Farther on I met two stout fellows on horseback chattering gaelic, and soon after I passed through the village of Kincardine O Neal. About it the country is pretty, but on both sides almost desolate. By this time I was pretty tired. Porter or spirits I cannot bear in summer. I had eaten brambles by the way too, which I detest, possibly this might have contributed to my lassitude by causing nausea and great thirst. However that may be I was very tired. Some miles farther on I entered a cottage to ask a drink of water, hoping that I might get milk, but the honest folk were sitting at a small table eating their dinner - and so I contented me with asking how far

Aboyne was distant. My lassitude increased and it was not without limping that I got here about half past seven. It is now after nine and I have eaten a poor supper and taken a glass of whisky and some water, and now I must return in mind to Aberdeen.

(At this point in the journal MacGillivray made a list of the plants he had seen during the day. This list is reproduced in the Appendix. It is divided into the plants seen in different sections of the walk during the day, and recorded as plants in and out of flower. He wrote until 11 pm when his candle burned down and completed the list of plants early next morning before setting off).

The trees will be mentioned afterwards. Once for all it is intimated that the names used are those of the Compendium Flora Britannica, auctore Jac Edw Smith Eq MD Londini 1816; and that the plants are arranged in the order of occurrence. At Mary Culter is a Den or Hollow in which runs a stream, well known to the botanists of Aberdeen, as furnishing several very rare plants, in particular the Herb Paris, Mountain Globe-flower, Sweet Woodruff, and Wood Crowfoot. It is named Corby Den and is, I believe, about seven or eight miles from Town. On the pebbly beaches by the river on the Peterculter side, opposite Corby Den are found the Sea Campion and Alpine Lady's Mantle, the latter probably being washed down the river from Braemar, being an alpine plant. In this neighbourhood the Cowslip and Early Purple Orchid grow in their proper season, both rare about Aberdeen. About a mile farther up and on the Peterculter side I observed another large den, well wooded, and to appearance a good place for plants. This, I suppose, is the bed of the stream which runs out of the Loch of Skene. There are no other Dens worthy of notice, even to this place, excepting perhaps that near Banchory where the salmon leap is. The birds observed between the Bridge of Dee at Banchory Davenack, and Banchory Ternan are the Magpie, Skylark, Woodpigeon, Pied Wagtail, Rook, Swallow, Chaffinch, Wheatear, Meadow Pipit, Blue Tit, Greenfinch, Heron, Robin, Wren, Blackbird, Hooded Crow, Goldcrest, Song Thrush, Linnet, Yellow Hammer, Partridge, and a bird resembling the Wheatear, which I have never yet got. The birds seen between Banchory and Charlestown were Magpie, Robin, Hooded Crow, Coal Tit, Yellow Hammer, Linnet, Hedge Sparrow, Meadow Pipit, Chaffinch, Rook, Pied Wagtail, and Woodpigeon.

Last night I bedded at eleven. I had a severe headache and a violent fit of shivering followed by a great heat but without sweating. I did not rest very well and so lay in bed till eight. I am now tolerably well only that I have got a catarrh, which I had before leaving Aberdeen. The names of birds to be found in my list are those of the Thirteenth Edition of the Systema Natura of Linneus. All day yesterday the weather was very fine.

Castletown of Braemar   Thursday 9th September

After breakfasting at Charlestown, in the Aboyne Arms Inn, and delivering into the right hand of the maid, who bye the bye, was a great and awkward lump and could scarcely apprehend what I said to her because I did not speak Scotch, three shillings sterling, or as a Scotchman says when in a grudging mood, three fyte shillings, being the sum demanded as a just and equitable remuneration for my entertainment and lodging, warn my readers not to think that I am ignorant of the construction of a sentence, or that I cannot distinguish tawdriness from elegance, but to understand that I am pleased to be facetious, as poor old what-do-ye-call-'em used to say to the Master of Ravenswood, I adjusted my portables upon my hump, walked out, and continued my journey. What a noble sentence! On counting my clinkum, by the way, previously to imprisoning it in my great chamois purse, I found to my great vexation that somehow I had lost sixpence! Charlestown is 30 miles from Aberdeen. It is a small village pleasantly situated on a plain not far from the river, and partially enclosed by hills. Near the 32nd milestone I went to the side of the river which here was close upon the road with the intention of looking for plants. I found the Yellow Mountain Saxifrage, Alpine Lady's Mantle, Sea Campion, all alpine. Besides these I observed the Common Lady's Mantle, Common Yellow Bedstraw, White Water Bedstraw, Purging Flax, Kidney Vetch, Wild Thyme. By a fountain near this I found the Yellow Mountain Saxifrage. I returned to the highway. I now found myself at the commencement of a large heathy plain bounded on all sides by hills of considerable height, with a small opening or pass straight before me, at the farther extremity. To the southwest I saw two very lofty mountains at the distance of about eight miles. Here there was very little natural wood, and scarcely any by the river. The subject of wood however in as far as it is connected with the river, will be separately treated. The Red Bear-berry was common on the moor. Its berries are bright red, very dry or almost mealy, and having an astringent and at the same time sweetish taste. The leaves have also an astringent taste, and are used in medicine principally as a diuretic. At the 38th stone I came to the river from which the road had separated at the 32nd. Here I found mountain scenery in true style, and saw that the road led into a pass between the hills. Here is the commencement of the Highlands. The hills became more rugged and were in many places covered with loose stones. The general character of the hills in the lower part of Aberdeenshire is that they are dull, uniform, clumsy masses, with rounded outlines, smooth without rocks, and covered with short heath. Here the appearance of the hills was different. They still retained their rounded figure, but were almost covered with loose stones, and had a few rocks though of in considerable size. At the commencement of the pass there was a good deal of natural wood, principally birch. In it I found a dead mole, the only wild quadruped seen since I left Aberdeen. Moles are not to be found in the whole of Scotland. In the whole Long Island consisting of Lewes, Harris, North Uist, Benbecula, South Uist, and Barray, with a multitude of smaller islands there are none. The same is said of all the other isles excepting Bute or Islay, I cannot recollect which. Lightfoot however makes the remark and it may be seen in his Flora Scotica. A mile farther on I saw a high mountain in the distance, which according to a woman of whom I asked its name is called Cairn o' Morven, or Mount Mar. Soon after I entered a plain in which I saw a village, and looking to the left recognised Pannich Lodge in which I breakfasted one morning with Mr Craigie when returning from a journey in the south in 1816. Near the village is a bridge over the Dee, named after it Ballater Bridge. It consists of five arches, the central of which is the largest. I am now fully convinced of the superiority in regard to beauty of equal arches, over those which increase to the central. By this bridge I crossed the river and proceeded along its southern bank. As you enter the Pass of Ballater, it seems a plain encircled by mountains but when above the bridge you find that it communicates with two other vallies in one of which runs the Dee, and in another a large stream over which the road passes. About the 45th milestone I entered a valley bounded by lofty mountains in which was a natural forest of Fir upwards of two miles in length. The soil was in some places very thin, and there the roots ran along the surface. One root I found to be 22 feet in length, measured by my own foot which is 10 inches. At the upper end of this wood there was a considerable quantity of Birch, and in it the Bilberry and Red

Whortle-berry were common. Hitherto the weather had been very fine, but now it began to rain, and continued until sunset. As I passed Abergeldy I learned by the clock on the tower that it was past five. The country was now completely highland, and the scenery was tolerable, but by no means of the higher order, as the hills were not high enough to be sublime, and too uniform and clumsy to be beautiful. It is remarked by Stewart in his Scenery of the Grampians that the pre-eminence in beauty of Benlomond over all the Scottish mountains is caused by it having incurvated outlines. None of that kind are to be seen here. The most predominant feature in the Scottish hills is roundness of outline which produces a disagreeable clumsiness. I know but few exceptions to this character. Benlomond and Culin in Skye are the principal: the former bending inwards in its outline, the other a vast mass of black and naked rocks, forming a summit of several miles in extent, composed of irregular peaks, which have the appearance of pyramids. At sunset the rain ceased. The country was now well wooded along both sides of the river. The trees were chiefly Birch. After travelling two hours in darkness I arrived here about half past eight.

On the heath between Charlestown of Aboyne and the Pass of Ballater I observed the following plants; first those in flower. (This list of plants is given in the Appendix). The birds seen were Skylark, Pied Wagtail, Meadow Pipit, Woodpigeon, Chaffinch, Rook, Hooded Crow, and Robin.

Near the 39th stone, and at the Bridge of Ballater, and near the 43rd stone I found a species of Rumex (Docks and Sorrels) growing which is not in Smith's Flora. Its name I cannot recollect. It was formerly used in medicine and might on that account have been cultivated and afterwards run wild. In the locality at Ballater Bridge it appeared to be growing naturally. *(In the journal at this point, presumably at a later date, MacGillivray has added in brackets Chenopodium bonus henricus - Mercury Goose-foot or Good Henry)*

Friday 9am

Last night I was lulled to sleep by the roar of waterfalls. I had a comfortable bed and slept soundly. Today I rose about eight, perfectly fresh, and taking a towel, razor, soap, a toothbrush and a pair of scissors from my knapsack together with a looking glass from the wall of my bedroom, proceeded to a stream of considerable size which runs near the Inn, and joins the Dee a little farther down.

Here I first shaved and then stripped and washed. After this I returned to the Inn, and now let me finish my narrative of yesterday's journey which I was obliged, partly by lassitude and partly by cold to leave off last night. It is certainly hard work to travel all day, and sit in wet clothes four or five hours into the evening composing and writing an account of the achievements of the day. Between the 44th milestone and the 49th or perhaps a mile or two nearer this the birds seen or heard were Magpie, Wren, Coal Tit, Goldcrest, Chaffinch, Treecreeper, and Woodpigeon.

The Coal Tit and Goldcrest keep together in flocks mingling with each other, and not infrequently the Treecreeper is found along with them. The last however, is not gregarious. They are common in Fir woods, seldom seen in any other. As I was cleaning myself today in the river near the Inn I observed a bird of the Dipper species plunging very frequently into a rapid part of the stream. This bird is not in the least web-footed, yet dives with great agility. Linnaeus makes it a thrush, others consider it as a starling. In my opinion it is neither the one nor the other, but of a distinct genus hitherto unnamed. It is certainly a curious bird, having the habit of a waterfowl, with the form of a land one; and to those who hunt after connecting links, might be an intermediate one between land and water birds. The Zig-zag Trefoil I saw near Ballater, and again in the woods on this side of Abergeldy to appearance not very rare. The Tender Three-branched Polypody and Prickly Club-moss I found near Abergeldy. The Yellow Mountain Saxifrage and Alpine Lady's Mantle grow by the roadside above the 48th milestone. Near this last place I found what I take to be the Spignel but of this I am not certain as the plant was out of flower. Common Yellow Cow-wheat occurred in the woods but regarding it I entertain some doubts. The plant however must be either the Common Yellow Cow-wheat or the Wood Cow-wheat. I had added some plants to my store since I left Aberdeen. Yesterday morning I examined* the Biting Persicaria found near Black's Brewery at Aberdeen, and the Cross-leaved Bed-straw found by Dee five miles above Upper Banchory. Today, or rather just now I have examined the Prickly Club-moss, Tender Three-branched Polypody picked up yesterday. All these excepting the first two I had known before, only I had not methodically examined them.

---

* Examining in this sense means making a detailed comparison of a plant species with the published description, for example, the number of petals, sepals and other anatomical features.

For the sake of unity and perspicuity I might be tempted to defer my account of the wood along the river until I got to the source, but as then I shall be in a wild and uninhabited country I must use expedition in travelling and will not have convenience for writing or examining notes. On this account I proceed to the subject without delay. From the mouth of the river to Upper Banchory there is very little natural wood. A few specimens of Common Alder are found here and there in the parishes of Nether Banchory and Maryculter, and in Maryculter and Peterculter some trees of the Bird Cherry and Blackthorn species are to be seen. About two or three miles below Upper Banchory the river is thinly fringed with stunted trees of Common Alder which continue with interruptions to Banchory, where there are also other species. Common Birch, Common Hazel, Blackthorn and perhaps others. The Common Birch had been seen for two or three miles farther down. It was principally to be found however at the mouth of rivulets entering the Dee. For two miles above Banchory there were considerable quantities of Common Birch, Common Alder, Common Ash, Common Oak and Common Holly. From five miles above Banchory to Kincardine there was little or no wood along the river. At a little distance from it however near the 25th milestone and the Bridge of Potarch there is a wood of Common Birch and a few trees of the same on the other side of the river. The Common Alder occurs here and there for several miles beyond this. In the space between Charlestown and the pass mentioned there is very little wood by the river, but at the upper end of the valley a considerable quantity along the hills. Common Birch, Common Oak and Common Ash are the species which occur here. In a country like this it is not easy to distinguish between natural and planted Fir. Little or none of this species had hitherto appeared that I could all indigenous. In the Pass of Tulloch there was a good deal of wood principally Common Birch, interspersed with Common Oak, and Common Hazel. At Pananach there is a great quantity of Scotch Fir but it appeared to be planted. At Ballater Bridge there is a little wood near the river of the species already mentioned. At the 44th stone the road was at a distance from the river. Here I saw Common Birch, Common Alder and Common Hazel in abundance. At 45 begins a planted forest of Pinus albies extending for about two miles along the road in a deep valley. At its upper part it is mixed with Common Birch and some others. From this to Castletown of Braemar there is a great deal of Common Birch and Common Alder but as I travelled over the greater part of this space in darkness I cannot say anything regarding it with precision.

I forgot to mention that near 43 I examined the Common Reed which I found in a small marsh. I have determined to remain here today, not for the sake of resting myself, as I shall prove in the evening, but of observing the peculiarities of the place.

Friday, past ten pm.

As I was returning from the river in which I washed this morning I observed the rocky summits of a mountain in the north towering above the intermediate hills. This, thought I, is in all likelihood the highest mountain here, I shall go to its top. It was at least twelve o'clock before I set out. Travelling toward the Dee which I had to ford, along the river which runs through the village I noted the following plants. They are such as grow exclusively by the river -

Sneeze-wort, Mountain Globe-flower, Colt's-foot, Wood Crane's-bill, Great Wild Valerian, Common Golden-rod, Cross-leaved Bed-straw, Rough-bordered Hawkweed, Alpine Lady's Mantle, Spignel, Common Lady's Mantle, Perennial Mercury, and Tufty Hair-grass.

In the cultivated fields I observed the Common Bush Vetch, Field Mustard, Corn Mint, Sun Spurge, Corn Spurrey, Sheep's Sorrel, Oat-like Soft-grass, Common Knot-grass, Spotted Persicaria, Annual Knawel, Common Hemp-nettle, Common Groundsel, Corn Sow-thistle, Silver-weed, Common Chickweed, Marsh Woundwort, and Common Rye-grass.

In the pasture grounds which occurred I observed the following - Common Ragwort, Devil's-bit Scabious, Purging Flax, Wild Thyme, Black Knapweed, Common Purple Clover, Autumnal Hawkbit, Dog's Violet, Pansy Violet, Ribwort Plaintain, Common Tormentil Septfoil, Upright Meadow Crowfoot, Common Yarrow, Meadow-sweet, Common Yellow Bed-straw, Common Burnet-saxifrage, Kidney-vetch, Hoary Plaintain, Common Bird's-foot Trefoil, and Alpine Lady's Mantle.

In waste places I found the Great Nettle, Cow-parsley, Broad-leaved Dock, Curled Dock, Spear Thistle, Mugwort, and Cock's-foot-grass.

I forded the Dee above its junction with the river which I had followed. On an island I found the Stone Bramble which I do not remember to have seen before. In case I might possibly be mistaken regarding it I noted the following marks - Rubus foliis ternatis, foliolis rhombeo-ovalis, duplicato-serratis, subtus pilosis, flagellibus longissimus herbaceis, acinis magnis coccineus paucis.

(This is the formal way of describing a plant species, using Botanical latin).

The berry was subacid and agreeable - I ventured to eat a number of them upon the faith of the aphorism; the fruits of the Class Icosandria are all eatable.

(The plant Class Icosandria includes cherries, pears, brambles, strawberries etc).

On reaching the north bank I obtained a view of the valley and of the Castle. Braemar Castle is situated at the entrance of the plain between the Dee and a mountain about half a mile distant from it. It stands upon a small mound. In its structure the ancient and modern styles are combined, it being a square house with a slated roof of the common kind, furnished with small circular towers at the angles. These towers are discontinued about halfway down. It is defended by a wall. This is a noble situation for the castle of a feudal chief. The scene reminds me of the tales of other years when from the castle of his forefathers the 'hunter of the deer strode to his hills' or the highland warrior issued to the raid of the Saxon vallies. The scenery here is in my estimation very fine. Those however who look chiefly to fertility of soil, and who would prefer the scenery of Holland to that of Switzerland, might pronounce it in no degree interesting. About one mile below the castle, and on the opposite side, is Invercauld at which there is a fine modern house, very pleasantly situated on a bank near the river. Here is a good deal of wood, principally Fir, and to appearance planted. In a wood on the north side of the river I saw a small covey of the black grouse, the Tetrao tetrix of Linnaeus. On looking to the course which I followed yesterday I found that I had passed a very high mountain not more than five miles from Castletown. Travelling on to the northward I came to a deep gullet or den in which I saw some trees of the Mountain Ash, Aspen and Common Birch species. I followed the course of the stream which ran in this den for several miles. It came from between pretty high hills which concealed the great mountain from my view. For a mile or more up this stream I observed the following plants, a mixture of alpine plants with those of the vallies;

Alpine Lady's Mantle, Common Rush, Common Bird's-foot Trefoil, Common Lady's Mantle, Lesser Spear-wort, Small Upright St. John's-wort, Stone Bramble, Common Marsh Marigold, Common Milkwort, Colt's-foot,

Devil's-bit Scabious, Spear Thistle, and many others.

Further up the valley through which came the stream I found a considerable quantity of White Birch. These trees had an aged and withered appearance. Many of them had fallen and I could not look upon their leafless trunks lying in different directions along the sides of the mountains without feeling a disagreeable sort of melancholy. I even felt the chill of horror run along the skin of my head and bristle my hair. I remember to have been similarly affected twelve years ago, by a similar sight when passing through Rosshire accompanied by my trusty squire Donald Dingwall, on my way to Aberdeen to enlist under the banners of Habby Macpherson (the Head-master of Aberdeen Grammar School). In a rut near the upper end of this valley I found the Chickweed-leaved Willow-herb, new to me, which I examined. The Common Grass of Parnassus occurred here also. The Red Whortle-berry was very common in this track and I ate a great quantity of the berries which are very acid and agreeable. The Bilberry was also frequent. Its berries are not acidulous. The Common Cow-berry was not so large as it commonly is on the plains but its berries were here at least double their normal size. In one place I found a large quantity of them, and filled my glass with their juice which I obtained by squeezing them in my handkerchief. "Come give us a toast," said I "Every man his own humours!" It was a most delicious draught. I would not have exchanged it with a bottle of the best wine that France ever produced. Let the epicure boast that he has drunk of the vintage of a thousand hills. I have quaffed the juice of the mountain berry of my native land amid her wildest scenes, where the bloated sons of sloth, the pampered swine of the south do not show their Saxon faces. My little glass, bye the bye, is very useful, for I have drunk a great quantity of water today and yesterday. Whither I be cold or hot, shivering or sweating, it does me no harm that I can perceive, and I naturally wonder at the stories of people falling dead after drinking cold water. I know no beverage half so good. When I got to the upper extremity of the deep valley which I had followed I got a view of the great mountain and descending from the eminence on which I then was I came to a stream which flowed by its base separating the mountain on its southern side from the others which surrounded it. The plants which I had observed between this rivulet and the Dee were the following;

Common Ling, Wild Thyme, Northern Hard-fern, Sweet Gale, Red Whortle-berry, Common Brake, Sheep's Sorrel, Mountain Ash, Marsh Arrow-grass, Bilberry, Aspen, Round-leaved Sun-dew, Common Yellow Bedstraw, Common Birch, Dwarf Birch, Bog Asphodel, Smooth Heath Bed-straw, Prickly Club-moss, Spear Thistle, Common Grass of Parnassus, Common Butterwort, Heath-pea, Pale Smooth-leaved Willow-herb, Needle Green-weed, Common Yarrow, Stone Bramble, Mountain Bramble, Common Tormentil Septfoil, Sweet-scented Spring-grass, Mat-grass, Mountain Cudweed, Small Upright St. John's-wort, Wood Horse-tail, Common Crow-berry, Cross-leaved Heath, Common Heath, Moss Rush, Red Bear-berry, Female Shield-fern, Wood Horse-tail, Common Fox-glove, Long-rooted Cat's-ear, and the Tender Threebranched Polypody. N.B. The plants in this list do not follow the order of occurrence as in the others, but are placed promiscuously.

Crossing the stream which separates the great mountain from the others I ascended a gravelly slope by its side. On this slope I found among other plants the Smooth Heath Bed-straw, Dwarf Alpine Cudweed and Foxglove. The Dwarf Alpine Cudweed was new to me. When I had reached the summit I sat down to consider how I should proceed. The mountain I divided into three portions; 1st, a plain rising gently at the farther end with a pretty rapid acclivity terminating about one third up in the stoney part of the mountain - 2nd, all the rest to within three or four hundred feet of the summit consisting of stones or gravel with some vegetation interspersed - 3rd, the remaining portion, similar to the last but more sterile. Like the surrounding hills the mountain was rounded in outline, excepting in one part where there was a rocky corry or hollow from the summit to about half way down. Hitherto the weather had been clear. Clouds now began to gather and to involve the summits of the distant mountains. They had not yet reached this however, and I had the hope of a magnificent view from the summit. So I began to ascend. In a valley to the west of the mountain was a forest of pine, to appearance natural. The plants which occurred in the first division were; Common Ling, Common Cotton-grass, Moss Rush, Red Bear-berry, Bog Asphodel, Common Juniper, Scaley-stalked Club-rush, Common Butterwort, Bilberry, Cross-leaved Heath, and Fir Club-moss.

The soil was peat, in which the roots of old fir trees frequently occurred as in the other moors of Scotland. On entering the second region I found the heath and other plants greatly decreased in size, but this arose solely from want of soil, for in places where it was pretty deep, they retained their former size, or were even larger than in the former part of the mountain. The plants which occurred in the lower part were; Common Ling, Red Bear-berry, Fir Club-moss, Northern Hard-fern, Bilberry, which was rare and without fruit, Common Crowberry, rare and without fruit, and Wavy Hair-grass in tufts here and there, and of great size.

Near the summit I sat down among stones and when I rose, a large covey of Ptarmigan or White Grouse sprung from the stones about 150 yards beneath one. These are among the most beautiful birds which I know. Near the summit, I should have said, of a projecting mass of the mountain which reached nearly halfway up where I found the Two-flowered Rush occurred. The stones on the hill which were coarse granite were not very much rounded but that in most places they had been frittered away into a coarse sand which had no vegetable covering. About the middle of this division, and about halfway up the hill commenced the Alpine Lady's Mantle and Common Juniper, that is in dry parts, for in the rivulets the Lady's Mantle is found in all the valleys. The Savin-leaved Club-moss grew here abundantly, on the ridges and gravelly places vegetation was scanty and dwarfish. In the hollows however it was more luxuriant. By a rivulet which ran here grew the Alpine Lady's Mantle, Smooth Heath Bed-straw, Dwarf Alpine Cudweed, Northern Hard-fern without fruit, another fern which I took for the Female Shield-fern, small and without fruit, Alpine Willow-herb. At the termination of this division and about 500 yards from the summit the plants were Common Crow-berry, stunted and without berries, the Cow-berry and Bilberry, both stunted and without berries, Least Willow, very abundant, Fir Club-moss, of the common size, Savin-leaved Club-moss, also of the usual size, Alpine Lady's Mantle, rare, Three-leaved Rush, common, a viviparous grass which I could not determine, Wavy Hair-grass, common but diminished in size, Smooth Heath Bed-straw, rare, Dwarf Alpine Cudweed, common. In the third region the surface was covered with stones. A few mosses and lichens appeared here and there. In some places were the Alpine Lady's Mantle, Fir Club-moss, Wavy Hair-grass, Dwarf Alpine Cudweed, and Curled Brake, the last very abundant and with perfect fruitification. Near the summit I found a single specimen of the Common Thrift still in flower. On reaching the summit I found it to be a long broad rounded ridge covered with stones, some of which were rounded, others angular. There were a few mosses and one species of Sedge. The scene which presented here I considered at the time as the most noble without exception which I had ever seen. On all sides, on the south, north, east, west, mountains appeared behind mountains with their rocks, ridges, and vallies. A solemn stillness reigned over the whole. No animated form was to be seen. The clouds rolled their dusky wreaths along the ridges. There is some incomprehensible, astonishing, melancholy, yet pleasing idea associated with the contemplation of a vast, almost boundless, solitary scene, over which desolation and sterility predominate with savage grandeur. I felt something pleasing yet repugnant in the idea of being a lonely hunter on these majestic wilds, yet I think there is a nobleness in it which does not associate itself with the image of a weak effeminate citizen. Certain it is that a highlander despises a citizen much more than a citizen despises him. Hence the natural superiority would appear to belong to the highlander. This however admits of differing explanation, but I have scarcely time to think, much less to express ideas. These three pages beginning with the words 'crossing the stream' were written this morning Saturday the 11th. I had neglected to prefix a date to them. It is now about nine o'clock and I defer the rest of my account till after breakfast.

Saturday 11th September about 10 am

I return to the summit of the great mountain. The scene as I have said was wild and desolate, but majestic in a high degree. The summits of the loftier mountains were involved in mist. Fortunately the clouds had rolled to the west from the mountain on which I stood and left its summit free. The beams of the setting sun darted here and there through the clouds which exhibited a hundred varying shades. In one place a vast livid mass hung over the ridges of a mountain, beautifully tinged in its lower fringed margin with deep crimson. In another the white vapour which clung to the summits of the mountains, assumed, where opposed to the sunbeams a roseate hue of the greatest delicacy. No wood appeared in the vallies, excepting here and there along the course of the Dee. From a small lake in a rocky corry at the distance of five or six miles, a white streamlet trickled down an alpine valley bounded by precipitous rocks. In the west through an opening of the clouds I saw a range of lofty mountains rising behind each other, the most distant being according to my estimation about 50 miles off. To the west and north-west the mountains continued undiminished in size as far as the eye could reach. To the east they diminished rapidly. The general character which they bore consists of roundness of outline, with here and there rocks and corrys, and sterility dependent upon the stony or gravelly nature of the surface. Descending a little from the highest point of the summit I proceed eastward for about half a mile till I came to a corry facing the south. Down a rapid slope about the middle of this I descended with as great expedition as I could manage, it being by this time after sunset. One side of this corry consists of an immense mass of white granite. I thought how ridiculously insignificant the most magnificent works of man are compared with this prodigious mass. What, said I aloud, are all the pyramids in the world compared with this mountain. Twilight was approaching fast, and when I got to the slope at the mouth of the corry I began to run. Here some large red grouse occurred, and a little farther down I saw two does, or females, of the Cervus elaphus species, the Red Deer. As I approached the stream which I have mentioned as separating the mountain from the others, I heard in a valley above several short brays or grunts. They increased in loudness and frequency, and to tell the truth appeared almost terrific. It was now dark, and I was surrounded by aweful mountains, without even a footpath to follow, and at least seven miles from any house. I knew there were no wild animals in Scotland which I had occasion to dread. The idea of the sound proceeding from some supernatural entity was not harboured for a moment. I knew that the stag bellows at a certain season but that season is the latter end of autumn. Besides, I was not well acquainted with his roar, having only heard one in the Island of Harris on an occasion similar in every respect to this, and according to recollection it was different from the cry which I now heard. I proceeded, recrossed the river and ascended a low ridge in the direction of my former route. Here I fell in with a sort of footpath, which I followed till I came over a deep glen which I recognised. About a mile farther on I found that I was too high on the side of the mountain that formed one side of the dark and fearful valley, and descended with difficulty about a quarter of a mile till I came to another footpath much more distinct than the upper. This path led me to the place where I had seen the mountain-ash, polar and birch on the rivulet. In this course I put my glass to frequent use. I lost the path several times but always found it again - and at length I got to the Dee, where I could distinguish the Castle. For two hours I had walked in darkness. The moon now began to show an indistinct light over the shoulder of a mountain, and Jupiter beamed brightly in the south. At length I found a place where the river was fordable, and at half past nine, as the landlord told me, I reached the Inn, where I found my bed occupied, probably because the people had not expected my return. Wearied as I was, I sat until about one o'clock writing. Today I rose about seven and felt the effects of yesterday's expedition in my knee joints which were very stiff. After breakfast I ascended the hill which is near the castle, and found that my mountain of yesterday is not that whose summit is seen from the Inn, but another farther to the north-west, a great deal higher. I omitted to mention in its proper place that the Moss Campion was frequent on the summit of the mountain, and that I found on its sides a plant which I take for the Cistus marifolius. This plant I had never before seen, and it had no flowers; but there is a certain affinity which is readily discernible by a person who looks minutely between plants of a family. I shall be much disappointed if this plant turns out to be any other. The description is this - Planta decumbens, suffiticosa, radix lignosus, caules divaricati, palmares, folia elliptica, obtusa, carina lata, involuta opposita, decussata-secunda, cortex cinerascens - and this, verily, is all that I can say about it. *

This, say I, is the proper way of studying botany - let who will say otherwise, the Fellow at Oxford or Edinburgh makes what he deems a glorious morning excursion among parterres (a formal ornamental flower garden) of blooming beauty - flowers I mean - with book in hand and perhaps 'spectacles on nose' - Shakesp. - or at least quizzing glass to eye, is just like a parrot chattering over the jargon of scientific nomenclature, without knowing anything more of the matter. Everybody is too conceited to think others can do better than himself. But I appeal to reason, and to my readers I remain here still today, for what purpose may be learnt from the next page.

---

* MacGillivray was disappointed. Cistus marifolium is now called Helianthemum canum, the Hoary Rock Rose. This plant is a European species found in a few very local sites in southern Britain. In MacGillivray's journal at this point he has added Azalea procumbens, 1830. This is the Trailing Azalea, now called Loiseluria procumbens, a plant found on Scottish mountains. Presumably MacGillivray realised his mistake in 1830, eleven years later, went back to his journal and added the note, a remarkable feat of memory and attention to detail.

The plants which this subordinate excursion has enabled me to add to my list are the following; Stone Bramble, Three-leaved Rush, Curled Brake, Chickweed-leaved Willow-herb, Alpine Willow-herb, Dwarf Birch, Dwarf Alpine Cudweed, and Wrinkle-leaved Willow.

Saturday night

About one o'clock, having finished my writing I took some paper, paints, pencils with me, and crossed the Dee by fording. On the north side opposite Castletown I found a noble place for a view of the Castle, Invercauld, the pass and its mountains - and so sat me down on the dyke of a kale yard at the back of the boatman's house. Finding my situation uncomfortable, I procured a wheel barrow and made it a very good substitute for a table. I first sketched the Castle and nearly finished it to my satisfaction, and then fell to the rest. I had made my drawing rather large and was obliged to leave out Invercauld. With this I was occupied till sunset when I again forded the Dee and returned to the Inn. I was informed by the boatman that the mountain which I had visited yesterday is named Beinn-na-buird, the other whose summits are seen from the village Beinn-a'an. The distance of its summit from Castletown is about 9 miles. As I have no botanical accounts for my readers tonight I shall try to patch up a story somehow or other. The most common incidents might be made interesting if looked upon through philosophical spectacles. My readers will recollect that I came here on a dark night, wet and weary. At the door I met a woman of whom I inquired if I might stay all night. Like other honest women of her kind she thought fit to scrutinise my exterior, in order to regulate her conduct by the result. So a candle was held to my face, and a door then opened for me. The result of my examination was not favourable to me for I was informed that I would be obliged to sleep with a man to whom she pointed in bed, and as I grumbled told me to consider the matter. To settle this weighty affair I was left to my meditations, an old hat, an old great coat, a large pack on my shoulders, a long bristly beard on my upper lip, for I am leaving moustachios, were all circum- stances unfavourable to a kindly reception. However I unloaded myself, and threw off my great coat, determined to remain and not despairing of a bed. I knew with what sort of animal I had to deal, and so produced a parcel of plants which I had in my hat and laid them together with some paper on the table. By this time the woman had returned so I asked a little spirits, not however from the mere inclination of drinking it. I was then ushered into another apartment and told that I might perhaps get a separate bed. For this intelligence I thanked my hostess. I ordered supper, when it came I found it miserable, oat bread, bad butter, two eggs and cheese. My bed however made up for the deficiency for it was very good. Next morning I was treated with a little respect and got a tolerable breakfast. I was questioned by one of the maids what use I made of my plants, and was seen writing a great deal. When I returned from the mountain last night, I found my bed occupied. I was told I might sleep in it however, and I replied that I did not care although I should. However I thought afterwards that I might look at another bed in the same room which was empty. It was far inferior to the other and was not made up. However I got into it and slept soundly. Today my landlady became very complaisant. I got an excellent breakfast, with honey superadded to the usual articles. When I returned in the evening, being very cold I ordered a little whisky. The landlady came and made me drink a glass of her own. She told me that tomorrow night I might stay at her father's, upon the supposition that I would be occupied all day drawing a fine cascade which she informed me is near his house. My supper tonight was greatly improved. I had ordered tea, and with it I got two sorts of bread, butter of superior quality and gooseberries. Besides we have got so very gracious that she has offered to go to her father's with me tomorrow to see that I may be allowed to stay there at night. Now although it is very desirable to have a good address and a good appearance, neither of which I have, it is perhaps still more so to have the quality of improving upon acquaintance, as it is termed. There is a way of managing matters, even in the most unfavourable circumstances, so as to produce the wished for result. And in common cases this is easily acquired, the only requisite thing being a little experience and a little deliberation. My treatment when on the West Coast will probably be similar to what it is here. Here I am taken for a vendor of books, there I shall be thought a petty pedlar. There is a nobility, as it is called, in the aspect and air of some people which ensures respect. This I have not, and never can attain. It is nothing but the sense of superiority expressed in the features and figure, and becomes habitual. What right has one man to command another, except by mutual agreement? Yet subordination appears to be natural, one man leads thousands, and every great enterprise or glorious achievement originated with one mind. I do not think that it is proper to assume authority, even when it might be done easily, and without apparent detriment to the party governed. A perfectly good man alone could be justified in so doing, but who has a right to assume power with such persuasion? Yet the desire of power appears to be very natural, at least it is very general. Most people feel affronted and indignant when the respect which they deem their due is withheld. A physician becomes haughty and sullen when taken for an apothecary, the soldier struts like a turkey cock when confounded with the mechanic, the shoemaker who has been taken for a taylor, perhaps blushes for shame, and the taylor despises the pack-merchant. All this arises from vanity, my great moral solvent. I remember the time, nor is it far distant when I had no small portion of this silly affection; but at present it makes little difference to me whether I be considered as a pedlar or a philosopher. Nor do opinions which are incorrect give me any uneasiness. I would much rather be good though universally esteemed vicious, than be high in the estimation of all men while harbouring corrupt inclinations. There is even a pleasure in being deemed less than one really is. At least there is a sense of exultation mingled with contempt, when a base action is ascribed to one, while he is certain that it never was done, and that it could not. On the other hand when an action is ascribed to good motives which had originated from bad, the actor if a man not utterly callous to the sense of propriety, or the dictates of religion, must feel the debasement of self condemnation, and out to blush if he heard attributed to him a noble action of which he knew himself incapable.

It is now 'witching time of night', the keystone of night's black arch. I am sitting by a window with a broken pane, without fire, without water, water of life, uisge-beatha, I mean, sickish and almost shivering with cold. It becometh me therefore to arise and to begin the work of a new week by tumbling into bed.

Castletown of Braemar   Sunday 12th   September 1819

I have been thinking of the etymology of the word whisky. Whisky is a corruption of the word uisge, the gaelic of water, uisge is used by abbreviation for uisge-beath, uisge-beath signifies either the water of life, or the water of birch, beath being used for a birch tree as well as for life, just as robur among the Romans denoted an oak and strength. The water of birch is the juice of that tree obtained by piercing the bark in spring, which it is well known was practiced of yore by the highlanders and according to Pennant and Lightfoot even in their time. This possibly was the drink used by the Fingalians at the 'feast of shells'. When the process of distillation became known the inebriating liquor obtained from malt was substituted for the sap of birch, and being used for the same purposes retained the name. So that the meaning of uisge-beath is not water of life, but water of birch.

Kingussie upon Spey   Monday 13th September

Yesterday about eleven o'clock I left Castletown of Braemar. About two miles from Castletown I had a delightful view of the valley of the Dee with Mar Lodge. About a mile farther is a fine cascade close upon the road. The river is not large, but there is a deep chasm extending nearly half a mile below the fall, well wooded and abounding in plants. The trees which I observed in this den were the Common Birch, Common Hazel, Mountain Ash, Bird Cherry, and Common Barberry.

Of other plants I observed the following; Rose-bay Willow-herb, Common Tormentil Septfoil, Common Polypody, Common Honeysuckle, Alpine Lady's Mantle, Cow-parsley, Raspberry Bush, Great Wild Valerian, Grey Poplar, Wood Crane's-bill, Common Bell-flower, Rough-bordered Hawkweed, Common Lady's Mantle, Broad Smooth-leaved Willow-herb, Hedge Woundwort, Common Golden-rod, Alpine Saw-wort, Sweet-scented Spring-grass, Germander Speedwell, Alternate-leaved Golden-saxifrage, Common Wood-sorrel, Herb Robert, Stone Bramble, Sweet Woodruff, Greater Stitchwort, Common Avens, Perennial Mercury, Devil's-bit Scabious, Common Primrose, Wood Strawberry, Meadow-sweet, Heath-pea, Tender Three-branched Polypody, and Colt's-foot. The Tender Three-branched Polypody is very common in Braemar. Rose-bay Willow-herb was very abundant in the Den. Near it I found a specimen of Little Quaking-grass.

Mar Lodge, a neat modern building, is situated on the north side of the river at the foot of a large wooded hill, 4 miles above Castletown. The plants noted between it and the Linn of Dee, 2 miles farther up are the following: Alpine Lady's Mantle, Small Upright St. John's Wort, Marsh Lousewort, White Water Bed-straw, Common Golden-rod, Common Marsh Marigold, Devil's-bit Scabious, Common Lady's Mantle, Spear Thistle, Alpine Saw-wort, Germander Speedwell, Great Nettle, White Trefoil, Upright Meadow Crowfoot, Broad-leaved Dock, Common Yarrow, Common Bell-flower, Marsh Woundwort, Long-rooted Cat's-ear, Small-flowered Hoary Willow-herb, Corn Spurrey, Dog's Violet, Common Butterwort, Common Hemp-nettle, Common Avens, Meadow Soft-grass, Corn Mint, Common Yellow Bed-straw, Common Sorrel, Greater Bird's-foot Trefoil, Sheep's Sorrel, White Trefoil, Common Wild Chamomile, Common Speedwell, Hoary Plantain, Broad-leaved Pond-weed, Common Tormentil Septfoil, Lesser Spearwort, Creeping Crowfoot, Floating Bur-reed, Yellow-rattle, and Marsh Thistle.

The woods were composed of the following species; Scotch Fir, Common Birch, and Mountain Ash. To these may be added the fructocose plants - Bilberry, Common Ling, Red Whortle-berry, Raspberry, and Common Crow-berry. The birds which occurred were very few. I only noted one species, the Chaffinch. About Castletown the Alpine Lady's Mantle appeared to be in its proper place, for upon the mountains it is not so frequent nor does it grow so luxuriantly. However it is to be found nearly to the summits of the lofty mountains.

About a mile from the Linn I passed a village composed of some of the most miserable huts which I have seen (Inverey). They were thatched with heather which added greatly to their melancholy-inspiring appearance. The Linn of Dee I had seen before in 1816. It is by no means interesting, consisting merely of a pretty large stream, dashing between rocks of no great height. At one place the breadth of the chasm is not more than four feet and here a person may leap over although there is some danger in returning because one side is higher than the other. The leap is trifling but the fury of the torrent boiling below makes it appear hazardous. I leapt over without disengaging myself from my knapsack or shoes, and not caring to leap up again with my baggage, I clambered up the rock and continued my journey. About two miles higher up the river, I entered a house to enquire concerning the source of the river. I was informed that it was near Cairngorm, but that I could not see it and get to Spey that night. The good man of the house who appeared to be a shepherd asked if I was hungry, and after I had answered that I was not, ordered his wife to give me some bread for the hills, which she did. A little above the Linn the woods end and no trees are seen above this. I continued my journey, although the shepherd had told me that I should be welcome to stay all night. About 3 or 4 miles above the Linn the Dee is joined by a river equal in size. I had explored the source of this stream in 1816 when I came across the mountains from Blair in Athol. Hitherto I had travelled in a westerly direction, but now proceeded northward following the river. There are no houses beyond the junction mentioned. About a mile above it I came in sight of a most magnificent rock, (The Devil's Point) with a mountain peak behind it of greater elevation. When I reached the rock I learned by the light scarlet colour of the clouds on the ridges that the sun was setting. Passing the rock I entered a valley bounded on both sides by very lofty and rugged mountains and terminating in a vast mass towering above the whole. Before I reached the upper end of this magnificent, though wild and desolate valley, night fell. Near the upper end of this valley the stream which I had followed separated into two. It was with great difficulty that I clambered to this part to see which was the largest that I might follow it. Having ascertained that the largest stream came from a valley which branched off at a right angle from the extremity of the main one, I entered this valley and proceeded about three quarters of a mile. It was by this time completely dark and I determined to rest myself.

Unfortunately I had proceeded so far up the glen which terminated high among the mountains that I had left behind me the region of heath, so that I could not procure enough to make a bed. However I got a sheltered place, and feeling warm after my exertions, thought that I might sleep all night without a covering of heath, as it was by no means cold. I soon found however, that the night air, mild as it was, chilled me and so I rose and pulled some grass and moss and spread them beneath me in a snugger place than that which I had before chosen. Melancholy ideas had been rising in my mind for upwards of an hour before this, but I contrived to repress them almost instantly. I knew that they could only add to the want of comfort to which my situation exposed me. I was never before aware that I could exert any control over these ideas, but now found to my satisfaction that I could completely suppress them. I endeavoured to compose myself to rest after eating some of my provision which consisted of a quarter of a barley cake and a few crumbs of cheese, and not feeling the most distant idea of danger, succeeded so far as to produce a sort of slumber between sleeping and waking. About midnight I looked up and saw the moon with some stars. They were at times obscured by masses of vapour which rolled along the summits of the mountains. I had now a better view of my situation. I was near the upper end of a high valley completely surrounded by masses of rock. Behind me in the west and at the upper end of the valley was a high mountain involved in clouds, on the right hand was another in the form of a pyramidous rock and contiguous with it a peak of less elevation, on the left hand a ridge running from the mountain in the west and terminating at the mouth of the valley in a dark conical mass, and straight before one in the east at the distance of nearly a mile, another vast mountain. The summits of all were at times enveloped in clouds. The wind which blew from the west was not keen, and the night was such as would be termed a warm one. Yet on wakening from my slumber I felt chilly, and soon after began to shiver. I then rose and gathered a few large stones, and a good deal of grass and short heath which I picked from among the stones. With these I formed a somewhat snug sort of bed or couch, and unloosed my pack and took a night-cap and a pair of stockings from it which I applied to their proper uses for my feet had been wetted and my hat alone did not keep my head warm. Then after eating some more of my scanty store and drinking two or three glasses of water from a rill which trickled near me I lay down, put heather and my knapsack over my feet, and placed myself in an easy posture, and fell asleep. I awoke fresh but weak this morning about sunrise, and put myself in trim to continue my journey. The stream which I had followed divided here into two, and I chose the largest. It led me to a magnificent corry in the form of a deep hollow scooped out of the great ridge on the left of the glen. The sides of this corry were composed of sloping rocks of vast height. The rivulets came tumbling down the centre in the form of a cataract. Here the rocks were most brupt but I had determined to proceed, at least to attempt the passage. Before I got to the base of the rocks I felt very weak and was obliged to stop every now and then. However I proceeded and found myself on the very summit of this vast mass of rock. It was covered with mist which rolled rapidly along the ridges. The sun now and then appeared through it. The view down the corry was delightful, dreadful it might have been to some. I had the whole glen, the corry, its rocks, and the opposite mountain with an alpine lake before me. The scene brought to my mind the lines in Beattie's Minstrel

> And oft he loved the craggy cliff to climb
> When all in mist the world was lost below

But here it was not the world below but the world above that was hid by the vapour. The scene was most sublime, and I contemplated it with great delight.

The plants which occurred in this corry were Dwarf Alpine Cudweed, Starry Saxifrage, Alpine Mouse-ear Chickweed, Alpine Meadow-grass, Savin-leaved Club-moss, Fir Club-moss. The Alpine Lady's Mantle in the higher regions had its leaflets split into three. Even here were specimens of the Sheep's Sorrel, but they were very small. The Common Bell-flower also occurred. The Rose-root I saw in a few places, it was very diminutive. The Two-flowered Rush was frequent also. Yet among these plants and at the very summit of the corry grew the Dog's Violet and Smooth Heath Bed-straw. I had now reached the rounded summit of the ridge, and proceeding along the streamlet which was the principal object of my research I traced it to two fountains and several subordinate ones. From the two principal founts I took a glassful which I drank to the health of four ladies of my acquaintance. Near the fountains I saw a covey of ptarmigans and a small bird I took for the Meadow Pipit. The only phenogamous plants (the modern spelling is phanerogam, and means the seed-bearing plants) which grew on the summit of the mountain were the Moss Campion and Least Willow, both in abundance. I gathered some specimens of the Moss Campion still in flower and of the Least Willow. Descending on the northern side of the mountain I came upon a precipitous corry down which I did not venture. Further on I came upon a precipice from which I had a view of a deep valley with a lake and a stream, ending in a plain partially covered with Fir. The country however appeared wild and dreary. The view from this place was vast, and I thought I distinguished the sea but of this I was not certain as the mist obscured the view at times. In my descent I saw a considerable number of ptarmigans and some specimens of crystallized quartz, though not very fine. On the northern side of the mountain some alpine lakes occurred in which I could not discover anything but Floating Bur-reed and a few poor specimens of Common Marsh Marigold. The Marigold I saw also in the rivulets. Holding still a northerly direction I crossed a broken plain and ascended a gentle acclivity, at the end of which I found a larger plain which I also crossed. Near the end of this plain I found, in a marshy place the Marigold still in flower, perhaps this may be a new species, but I saw no distinction excepting in point of size. At the end of this plain I came to an opening which led into a deep valley bounded by rocks and rapid gravelly slopes. I descended by this valley which I found very long and very rugged into a plain which led to a stream of considerable size, which I knew ran into the Spey.

During my descent I found the following plants; Alpine Lady's Mantle, Alpine Meadow-rue, Alpine Mouse-ear Chickweed, Broad-leaved Alpine Mouse-eared Chick-weed, Alpine Meadow-grass, Common Wood-sorrel, Tender Three-branched Polypody, and Curled Brake. Further down the Small-flowered Crowfoot occurred in full flower and great abundance. Near the mouth of the valley I saw the Sternus cinclus (Dipper) upon the stream which ran through it. After fording the river mentioned, I proceeded down the valley for about two miles, after this I turned to the north in the direction of the Spey. In this course I fell in with some houses. The good man of one of them was near and I proposed some questions to him relative to my course which he answered. I was also invited to enter his house where the good woman gave me a drink of milk. On hearing that I had been out all night they expressed their surprise and concern, and from what I learned of their conversation regarding it I found that the people of this country are not as hardy as they ought to be. To be a night among the mountains at this season of the year is surely a matter of no great concern and if I had a good plaid in which to wrap me I could sleep out at night without feeling much inconvenience. Leaving this place I proceeded toward Spey which I reached after a walk of four or five miles. I crossed it by boat, and entered Kingussie where I now am. In the dusk I began to feel very melancholy and to prevent this disagreeable sensation went out and fell in with an old man with whom I chatted for some time. I then returned, drank some toddy with my landlord, and wrote the greater part of this. Some remarks respecting the plants which occurred today may have been omitted. I shall see tomorrow. In the meantime I propose to have a good sleep.

Kingussie Tuesday morning

I slept soundly last night, though in a bad bed. I rose about eight, shaved, washed, and examined my plants which I had carried from the mountains. In the corry of the great mountain I found what I take for the Purple Saxifrage, and the Alpine Speedwell which although out of flower I could not mistake on account of the form of its leaves and capsule, the former being ovate, subserrated, smoothish, subciliated at the base, the latter elliptical and emarginate. The season for visiting the alpine regions is over, the plants by now out of flower. However I have done well since I got among them. This is a miserable looking village. It is situated on the north side of the Spey, which is here a large, still river, very unlike the Dee which is uniformly rapid in its whole course. Along the course of this river, there is a plain about a mile, or perhaps two, in breadth, stretching to a great distance both in an eastern and in a western direction from this village. To the south are low hills ending inn a vast range of mountains, running parallel with the river, those from which I descended yesterday. To the north and west are rugged mountains also of great elevation. The country appears tolerably fertile. The Gaelic language is spoken. This village is in the district of Badenoch in Invernesshire.

Fort William   Lochaber, Wednesday, 15th September, 1819

After breakfasting at Kingussie I continued my journey along a fine new road to Fort William. When I had proceeded a few miles I found the aspect of the country was beginning to change. Mountains and glens there were still in abundance, but rocks appeared here and there and the outlines of the mountains were more irregular than those of the hills of Aberdeenshire. Instead of the dull uniform heath which covers these hills, patches of verdure were seen among the rocks, and the Fir had completely disappeared. Fir woods in a level country are to me disagreeable, I might almost say intolerable. In a mountainous region of the ordinary kind it is still disagreeable. Only a few trees of the kind scattered among the faces or summit of the rocks have a fine effect. It is in mountain scenery of the first order that the Fir has its proper place. Being a gloomy tree, it adds much to the effect of sublime or vast scenes, but is by no means suited to those in which beauty or gaiety are predominant. It is in the latter case like an old melancholy matron frowning over the innocent mirth of a group of lively young girls. I remember with pleasure the noble effect which a forest of pines had upon the scenery of Loch Mari in Rosshire which consisted of rugged and in many places precipitous mountains of vast height enclosing a lake twelve miles in length and two in breadth. When I had proceeded about fourteen miles I saw some lofty mountains in the distance enveloped in clouds, and some miles farther on came to a beautiful lake of considerable size. At its farther end were the lofty mountains mentioned, having their summits hid among the clouds while patches of white vapour floated along their sides. The banks of the lake were well wooded and at its nearer end was a sandy beach. If Cumberland thought to produce anything more beautiful than this I am mistaken. On the beach I saw an eagle which I obliged to rise by hallooing, that I might discover the species, this however I did not effect, the distance being too great. The plants which occurred in this course were the same as those of Braemar. The Alpine Saw-wort grew abundantly, but I did not observe the Alpine Lady's Mantle or the Yellow Mountain Saxifrage. At the end of the lake I saw a considerable quantity of Rose-bay Willow-herb. When I had reached the mountains mentioned I found that I was only about the middle of the lake. Night was falling and I spoke to two men about an Inn. Fortunately one of them was the owner of a little public house at hand and conducted me to it. Here I was obliged to drink some whisky with the landlord and two men who were travelling from Spey to Fort William. I supped on porridge and skimmed milk, as nothing better could be got, and in due time went to bed. I rested very ill and lay in bed till ten this morning. I then breakfasted on bread and milk, paid my hostess and departed. The name of this place is Aberairder. It is situated at the base of high mountains, near the middle of the lake mentioned which is Loch Lagan. The lake is well wooded along its whole extent. Common Birch forms the principal part of the woods. The other trees which I observed were Mountain Ash, Common Oak, Common Hazel, Aspen and Common Holly. The Perennial Mercury was very common along the road. When I had reached the western extremity of the lake it began to rain. The river which runs out of the lake passes through a wild country for about 15 miles, and enters Loch Lochy about 8 miles distant from Fort William. For a great part of this course the road is within sight of the river. At one place it boiled through a narrow chasm which reminded me of the Linn of Dee, and at the lower part formed a fine cataract. When I was within twelve miles of this place the rain abated, and the shadowy form of Ben Nevis appeared among the clouds. As I proceeded the mist cleared up and my view of this majestic mass improved. The road winds round its base at the distance of a mile or two, and for several miles I had changing views of the vast rocks which compose it. Their appearance brought to my mind that of the hills of Cullin in Skye, and the mingled sensations with which I beheld the black pyramidal masses of which it is in many parts composed emerging from among the clouds. In the dusk I reached this place considerably fatigued. From Kingussie to Fort William is a distance of 48 miles. The birds which I observed in this tract were the following; Yellow Hammer,

Raven, Reed Bunting, Mallard, Crow, Sky Lark, Wheatear, Linnet, Chaffinch, Magpie, Woodpigeon, Meadow Pipit, Hooded Crow, Robin, Pied Wagtail, Whitethroat, and Dipper.

Besides these I saw several hawks, one eagle, a small bird with a red tail, and a species of tit larger than the Coal Tit or the Blue Tit. I also heard the Wren and Coal Tit. The proper name of this place is Inver-Lochy, being situated near the junction of the river Lochy and the sea. This is the name by which it is known to the highlanders. Inver and Aber are synonymous and are applied to places situated at the junction of a river with a lake or the sea, or with a larger river. Thus Inver-ary, Inver-ness, Inver-ury, Aber-brothick, Aber-deen, Aber-geldy. The River Lochy is here larger than the Dee near Aberdeen.

The inhabitants of the highland districts through which I have passed bear the same general physical character. The men are middle sized, robust but not fat, much less corpulent, yet by no means thin. Their features are very distinct from those of the lowlanders, bearing a peculiar wild, I might almost say harsh and rather savage expression. They are totally devoid however of the grinning distortion of the moveable features almost universal among the lowlanders of Aberdeenshire, and I believe of several other shires, and the ludicrous clogged motion of the legs accompanied with the heavy swing of the body which adds so much to the awkwardness of the lowland peasant, the highlander does not possess.

The great, if not the only, reason of this is that he does not load his shoes with a pound or two of iron nails. The young men of most of the Isles which I have visited move with as much agility, ease, and even elegance, as if they had been taught to pay an unremitting attention to all their motions. The nature of the country has perhaps some influence over this. The heavy trailing motion of the feet, proper enough in following a plough, or attending a dung cart, would never do for the propulsion of the cas-chrom or the cas-direach. Agility too is much more requisite in a mountainous country than in a plain one. The highlanders are peculiarly well adapted to military service, as is proved by their history. Their very appearance is highly indicative of this adaptation. But if the male part of the highland peasantry are superior in form, and agility to the lowlanders, the females are as far inferior in aspect of beauty to the lowland women.

They partake in a great degree of the harshness of features, and deep intermuscular lines which characterise the males - and these become indicative of qualities which do not correspond with our ideas of the female character. For the softness and delicate colouring of a lowland milkmaid it would be in vain to search the highlands or isles. Early exposure to labour and privations of different kinds gives them a firmness of frame which is not acquired even by the males of many countries. My remarks are only applied to the peasantry. The case is different if I consider the higher orders. Walter Scott has erred egregiously when he has made a tall thin form characteristic of the Gael. The short robust figure is by far the most predominant. It is this frame alone which can endure the hardships and fatigues at which the Highlander repines not, while the Saxon sinks under them. I have seen many thousands of Highlanders, and I never saw among them a single scrag but one, on the other hand I never saw but one corpulent highlander, and he was rendered so by being confined to his house by a diseased leg.

Fort William   Thursday night   16th September 1819

Today I rose about eight and looked through the town while breakfast was preparing. This is a small town or large village situated on the southern shore of Loch-eil, near the influx of the Lochy river. Its present English name is derived from the Fort in its vicinity. The highlanders in their own language call it by the original name Inbher-Lochi. After breakfast I left the Inn with the intention of visiting a friend, on whose top I had long wished to crow. So taking with me the Compendium of the Flora Britannica, some paper, and pen and ink, I entered Glen Nevis. This valley is bounded on the north-east by Ben-nevis, on the south-west by mountains of less elevation. A rapid stream runs through it, as is the case with every highland valley of considerable size. It is neither beautiful nor remarkably ugly. Ben-nevis adds nothing to its appearance for the summit of that mountain is not seen from it. I followed the course of the river mentioned for about two miles when I found myself halfway up the valley and opposite the middle of Ben-nevis. So I forded the stream and began to ascend the mountain on its southwest side. The weather was very fine - a tinge of frost was perceptible in the air and the tops of the hill were thinly covered with snow which had fallen under night. On reaching the apparent summit of the mountain I found that I was not much more than halfway so renewed my efforts - and at length found myself on the brink of a vast precipice, where a small cairn of stones indicated that this part had been considered the summit. Here I gave three faint cheers with my hat off. In a cleft of the rock here which had been used as a resting place I saw fragments of earthern and glassware, chicken bones, corks, and bits of paper, indicating that the visitors of Ben-nevis were commonly better provided with forage than I happened to be. At some distance from this place there was a larger cairn upon higher ground, and to it I proceeded. Here I managed to force out three faint cheers as at the other place. Faint I say they were and forced - because I had engaged with myself previously to my departure from Aberdeen to act so - and the free raptures of enthusiasm had nothing to do with constraint. Had it not been for this unfortunate engagement I dare say I had roared with all my might upon the summit of the highest mountain in Scotland. In regard to the height of this mountain I neither feel surprised or disappointed in expectation. I had not formed magnificent ideas of it, and I shall not be astonished till I see the Alps or the Mountains of the Moon in Africa, or of Nepal in Asia. Here however were some tremendous rocks, perhaps the highest which I ever saw. They formed the northeast side of the mountain, and were at least a thousand feet in height. It was almost terrifying to look down upon them from the summit. Patches of snow lay here and there in the vast chasms of these tremendous rocks. The upper fourth of the mountain is completely covered with grey stones of various sizes, from several feet in diameter to a coarse sand. Of course, there are scarcely any marks of vegetation in this part. The middle part on the side by which I ascended is composed of rocks in the chasms of which run several streamlets. The lower part is heathy and not very rugged. From the top I had an immense view. In the South, East, North and Northwest, mountains appeared without interruption. Only in the east they were lower, in the south they wore a very rugged and desolate aspect. Sharp pointed rocks, rugged corries, deep craggy glens, streaks of grey stones and gravel alternating, completed the scene. I looked for the highest mountains, such as Schiehallion, Benlawers, but none appeared greatly pre-eminent above its neighbours. Only Cruachan in Argyle I readily distinguished by its figure. I saw the lake by which I had passed on my way to this place, and to the north Loch Lochy, with its river, and part of the Caledonian Canal. The Isles which I could distinguish were Mull, Jura, Liss-more, Cannay, Rum, and others. In the direction of the Canal I thought I distinguished the mountain at the mouth of Invermoriston on Loch Ness. The hills of Skye I did not see, for clouds rolled here and there along the verge of the horizon. I descended by the south-west side, for a considerable part of the way in a ravine. When I had reached Glen-nevis the sun was setting and night was falling when I arrived at the Inn. (*At this point MacGillivray wrote a list of the plants he had seen during the day; see Appendix*, The plants seen while climbing Ben Nevis). The birds which I saw on the mountain were an eagle, a ptarmigan, several ravens, and two hawks.

The best proportions of the ingredients of whisky toddy are: one glass of good whisky, three glasses of hot water, two teaspoonfuls and a half white sugar. There is a secret and irresistible impulse that binds us to the scenes of our youth. In the most remote regions of the globe the mind dwells upon those scenes with delight - and almost all who have been obliged to undergo a temporary exile from their native land wish to return to it, and to spend the last years of their sublunar existence in the place where they first drew their breath. The remembrance of scenes of this kind was rising in my mind yesterday. I was coming into the vicinity of the Isles. I had friends there whom I loved. The mountains and lakes and heaths and rivers of that land, bleak and barren as it is, are dear to me, and ever will be. Was it then blameable in me to wish to spend a few days there? If mankind were utterly destitute of this attachment to localities many of the year's operations dependent upon sociality and concurrence of sentiment and operation could not be performed. I have often wondered how the poor islander clings to the barren rocks on which his forefathers lived, clings with a firmness of attachment which can only be destroyed by the barbarity of frozen-hearted landlords deaf to every call of humanity. And when at length after being forced from his paternal home, he reaches those western regions which lie beyond the vast ocean whose eastern margin washes the land of his youth, he bestows on his new possessions the names which awaken the sad and heavy remembrance of the days that were. I cannot dwell upon the idea, my eyes fill with tears when it presents itself to my mind.

I thought I could have become a citizen of the world, but I never shall. I know not what may be my fate - but I feel at this moment a glowing attachment to the land of my forefathers which almost outshines every other, and I am apprehensive that the worst dreadfulsome of mental diseases, nostalgia, will overwhelm me when in far distant climes. Yet begone I shall and must, for independence is scarcely to be attained here, and without it life would be miserable even though cheered by the smile of beauty.

Fortwilliam, Friday night, 17th September

It has rained incessantly today. This was not the cause of my delay however. The contents of my knapsack, particularly a parcel of plants which I have brought from Beinn-na-buird and Cairn-ghorm had got into confusion and it was necessary that I should reduce them to order before proceeding. I had my route also to determine, and had to get in perfect trim, that I might enjoy some pleasure on my journey; for without order I find that I can no longer expect pleasure. Tomorrow I shall proceed southwards. It is certainly somewhat singular that as yet I have been free of melancholy. In common indeed I have been so unremittingly employed in looking after plants and in writing, that melancholy could not possibly find an opportunity of obtruding. There have only been two points of danger, when I was benighted on Cairn-gorm, and today. On both occasions however I have escaped. Escaped I say, for I am actually beginning to hate pain. This is certainly a very wonderful change but I have not leisure or inclination to account for it at present. I wrought hard for the greater part of this day at my Braemar landscape. In the morning I visited the Fort, and in the evening a large burial ground in its neighbourhood. I had expected to find monuments erected to some of those poor fellows who fell in the days of Charles, but I was disappointed. This country is the birthplace of heroes. Here lived and fought the Camerons of Lochiel. The seat of the representatives of this celebrated family is, I am told, twelve miles from this, but upon the same Loch or arm of the sea, Loch-ial. In the original this word is tri-syllabic, Loch-i-al, the i being pronounced like the italic or the French one. And this undoubtedly Campbell has made it in his warning. The verse of this exquisite piece consists of eleven syllables, to which may be added a short one at the beginning, like the introductory note in a piece of music. Thus,

'Proud Cumberland prances insulting the slain;
1   2 3 4   5 6   7 8 9   10   11
and their hoof-beaten bosoms are rode to the plain'
1   2 3 4   5 6   7 8   9 10   11

This is the regular measure of the whole piece, and the rules of English versification do not admit the substitution of nine for eleven syllables in a regular piece. Therefore the first line of the poem has the same number of syllables as the others;

    Loch-i-eil, Loch-i-eil! beware of the day,

    1 2 3   4 5 6   7 8 9 10 11

nor could it possibly be

    Loch-eil, Loch-eil! beware of the day

    1   2   3   4   5 6 7 8 9

For although in poetry set to music, one syllable may be either prolonged so as to occupy the time of several, or repeated so as to fill up the measure, in poetical composition unconnected with music the measure must be complete, and absolutely so when rhyme is used. Now this piece which, although lyric in structure is essentially dramatic, was assuredly never intended to be sung. For with as much propriety may the Tragedy of Othello be set to music, or Cato introduced in a bobwig and red velvet (or plush) breeches singing his celebrated soliloquy. The error in pronunciation which makes the number of syllables nine originates in the injudicious mode of spelling the word used by Campbell and others. In no instance are the letters i-e-l separated into two syllables when occurring in a word purely English, or even Scotch, wield, shield, yield, chiel(d), biel(d). Therefore from analogy the word Lochiel ought to be disyllabic. But it is not the orthography, but the pronunciation in the original of the word that is to regulate the English pronunciation. As a similar example take the word Zoology, which from analogy ought to be trisyllabic, while attention to the original pronunciation makes it tetrasyllabic. The word ought, when introduced into the English language to have been written Lochiel, which would effectually have prevented mistake. Philology has put patriotism out of place, but I return to Cameron and the warriors of yore. I scarcely ever hear the names without thinking of Byron's third Canto of Childe Harold, and fancying that the 'war notes of Lochiel, savage and shrill' are whistling in my ear, or without wishing and hoping that days like those which are gone may yet appear when 'the plaided warriors of the north shall issue from their vallies to fight for their rights and liberties' Scott S of the S. I verily wonder how Fortwilliam could have stood so long here. I think forty swack chiels wi bottomless breeks might easily fling themselves over the wall on a dark night, and kick up a pretty shine. By the powers, I like the idea. Scotland and liberty for ever! 'We little band of brothers' if death and the three furies, how we should buffet the Saxons. But alack-a-day! I had almost forgot the good advice of the sage philosopher of beefsteaks and tea 'the use of travelling is to regulate imagination by reality'. I stand reproved. I also forgot for a moment that excepting on a few extraordinary occasions I consider all mankind as my brethren, and that on a few extraordinary occasions I would as readily hug a greasy Hottentot brother, as a Scotch cousin twelve steps removed. Now I say that upon the whole my voice is not for war, and that when perfectly sober, I consider war as the most absurd of all human conceptions. I must not be understood as speaking of sobriety as a winebibber would. It appears to me however that there are occasions on which recourse must be made to force, and one of those just occasions I conceive was that of the year forty-five. The representative of a family by whose hands the sceptre of Scotland had been swayed for centuries came poor, deserted and forlorn among the descendants of the loyal subjects of his ancestors. His enemy was upon the throne and his power extended even to the remote isles. Interest dissuaded the chieftains to arm, but compassion and the sense of duty overwhelmed every other motive. The highlanders armed in small bands, they joined their scanty forces, they marched, fought, conquered and were conquered. The sacred cause of liberty, for they fought for their king, their country, and their religion, was by their enemies branded with the name of rebellion. Proscription, confiscation, death, murder, rapine, all the brutal insolence of power followed. Can any Scotchman consider these things and feel his heart beat calm? Accused be the miscreants who deserted this country, but, I had forgot that men may be looked upon as a parcel of monkeys, who play the most ludicrous tricks, or like a set of puppets in a show set in motion by the strings of passion and prejudice. But this will not do after all, and I can only be so philosophical as this simply in idea. So by the blood of the martyrs of liberty, were such a scene to be acted anew, I would be among the first to cock my bonnet and shout, Albin gu brath!

King's House, Argyllshire, Saturday night, 18th September

About ten o'clock this morning I left Fort William and proceeded along the side of Lochial singing 'Lochaber no more'. The clouds had rolled away and the sun began to shine. For seven or eight miles the road kept near the loch. In all this course the scenery is uninteresting. The hills indeed are green, and not clumsy, but there is too much sameness and too little wood, and the shores of the loch are too regular. About seven miles down a series of lofty and beautiful mountains commence which stretch on the north side of the lake towards the isle of Mull. Here also on the north side a flattish point of land projects which marks the boundary between Loch Linne, the great expanse which commences at the Sound of Mull and Lochias, the part of the same arm of the sea which passes up to Inverlochy, and then turns and proceeds for about eight miles in a northwesterly direction. The principal direction of Loch-Linne and Lochias is in line with Loch Lochy and Loch Ness, two freshwater lakes, and in consequence with the Caledonian Canal, the western extremity of which terminates in Lochias near Inverlochy, as the eastern does in Loch Beauly, the upper part of the Murray Firth near Inverness. Opposite the point spoken of the road turns southward, bending a little to the east for several miles, till it terminates at the ferry of Loch-leven, a branch of Loch linne. About the middle of this part of the road I had a very fine scene. On my right hand was Loch-linne, bounded by the great mountains on its northern shores and the isle of Mull, and on its southern by the hills of Argylle. Straight before me, in the southeast was the opening into Loch-leven. The lake itself was not seen, but its place was marked by a vacuity bounded on the Argyll side by very beautiful green lofty mountains, wooded at the base and along their sides, and on the Lochaber side by hills farther retired and less elevated. The view culminated in a group of very rugged mountains far superior in height to the rest. There were some slate quarries by the road. At the mouth of Loch-leven there was a peat moss about half a square mile in extent, which was very deep, the peats having been cut five deep from it. On the opposite side in Argyll was a most beautiful green wooded valley, rising among the mountains. The tract over which I had passed was pretty well wooded in some parts, and by no means deficient in plants. The whole, excepting a few patches of cultivated land which occurred, was heath or rather hill pasture, the very mountains here being green unlike those of Aberdeenshire. The plants which occurred were the following: (see Appendix)

When I reached the ferry I saw a boat upon it the people of which cried to me, and afterwards took me in. The loch here was scarcely a quarter of a mile in breadth, and the stream being very rapid, resembled a river issuing from a vast lake. In the boat I found a fellow with whom I drank a little whisky in the Inn at Ballahulish on the other side. We proceeded about two miles together up the west side of Loch-leven till we came to the slate quarries where he left me. The scenery on the lake was very fine. There are several small islands in it. On one of them Eilean Mhunidh, or St Mungo's Island are the ruins of a small chapel and a burial ground. My companion informed me that formerly the people attending on the funerals went to the island and generally got drunk so that not infrequently some lives were lost on the passage back. To prevent this, he said, only four men were allowed to inter the body. A little above this island I entered Glencoe, celebrated for its massacre and awful scenery. For about two miles it has the common appearance of a highland valley, having some wood and being rather beautiful rather than otherwise. But upon turning to the eastward, at the end of this part of the valley, I saw before me on one side a tremendous mass of rock upwards of two thousand feet in height and on the other a long curved ridge of rocks little inferior in elevation to the great mass. In the bottom of the valley was a small lake, through which ran a stream of considerable size. By this time the sun had set and night was approaching fast. The valley did not equal my expectations and I was glad that I should have an opportunity of seeing it to advantage when the shades of night and some dark clouds which were approaching from the west should add sublimity to it. Before I reached the upper part of the glen, a thousand sparkling eyes were peeping from behind the clouds. I stood and looked back on the scene. A deep valley opening to the west, with a lake gleaming at its farther end, and its sides formed by majestic mountains. On one side three vast conical rocks, the abrupt terminations of as many mountain ridges, with their peaks and chasms and torrents; on the other a semicircular range of rocky mountains. The clouds rolled along the summits of the mountains, adding gloomy grandeur to the shades of night, and the faint light of the west only served to render the darkness perceptible, and to add by contrast to the horror of the scene. Yet I felt no horrific, gloomy or melancholy sensations, but felt disappointed that I could not prevail upon myself to be sad. At the upper end of the valley I met several who neither spoke nor were spoken to. Jupiter was by this time beaming in the south. He was the only object which attracted my attention for several miles, for on earth, mountains and rocks and rivers were indistinguishably blended. I was not to be sure in absolute Stygian darkness for I could readily perceive that I had still four fingers and a thumb on my right hand when I held it before me. But there is nothing interesting in the account of a nocturnal scamper of this kind, for I never have the good fortune to fall in with bogles or witches who might help me by a ride on the end of their broomstick. So about nine o'clock or so I got to the Kings Inn situated upon the heath in a dreary region, built I believe for the benefit of the King's troops in the time of the rebellion, as it is called. I write this on Sunday, having been obliged by sleep and cold and fatigue conjunctly and separately to leave off last night at the end of my list of plants. The birds which occurred between Fort William and Loch-leven ferry were of the following species; Wren, Robin, Linnet, Raven, Hooded Crow, Rook, Pied Wagtail, Meadow Pipit, Chaffinch, Yellow Hammer, Common Gull, and Blue Tit.

Tyndrum, Perthshire   Sunday evening   19th September 1819

About eleven o'clock I left King's-house Inn, and proceeded westward over a dreary tract of moor on which nothing interesting occurred till I came to Inverounan about nine miles on, where I found a lake two or three miles in length. Out of this lake runs the Urchay river which falls into Loch-awe, one of the largest lakes in Scotland. Near this lake I saw some Firwood. Crossing the Urchay by a bridge I pursued my course along a good turnpike road, and in the dusk arrived here. My journey of yesterday was twenty-nine miles. Today I have travelled only nineteen. I am not fatigued, and in truth have had little occasion to be so. But I shall make up for this before I get to London, unless I think proper to note the plants and birds which occur, which is one of the chief causes of my delay hitherto. My course of today has been over a wild, almost uninhabited district. Few trees occurred and few plants. The hills are in some places pretty high but not attracting. Yet one travels here with far different sensations from those which he experiences on the moors of Aberdeen or Morayshire. There the dull continuity of brown heath is disgusting. Here there is so much verdure everywhere that even in the most solitary parts one cannot feel sad or impatient. Autumn has not yet given her mellow tints to the mountain scenery. The freshness of the green is surprising and almost emulates that which marks the first efforts of vegetation in spring. The roads are very good. Only in a few places the torrents have cut them up. It is ridiculous in one who travels on such roads to talk of the wildness of the country over which they lead, as if he had surmounted obstacles. In regard to the fatigue of walking there is no difference between Glencoe and the Carse of Gowrie. The case was very different a hundred years since, and then indeed the Highlands might have been called rugged and desolate. The roads have destroyed the effect of many of the wild scenes. Glencoe for instance, loses a great deal of its horror to the traveller when he reflects that he is walking on as fine a piece of road as any in Scotland. To feel the full effect of its rugged nature it would be necessary to traverse it by the indistinct and interrupted path which one may fancy to have existed in it before the road was made. The Highlanders in the remote isles have not yet in many places a distinct conception of the utility of roads. Their own footpaths they consider in fact as roads, and roads perfectly sufficient too. The distinction of name between them is amusing. A footpath between two villages they call an rathad mor, which signifies the great road, a turnpike road in the same situation is named mor an right, the king's great road or highway. A small and indistinct path along the side of a mountain or to a shiel or such place is what they consider as a footpath. Thus the common footpath of the Englishman or Lowlander, the Highlander considers as a highway and walks with as much expedition and more agility upon it as the others do upon their turnpikes. On a turnpike road one doesn't fatigue himself much, but his feet, ankles and knees get sore and stiff. On a footpath again the reverse happens. The feet are comparatively easy but the body is more fatigued. To a person intending to travel far on a turnpike road I would recommend thick stockings and shoes with very thick soles and without heels. Among the hills again the best shoes are those of the Highlanders, made of half-tanned leather, very light and sewed so as to admit the water and let it out again. The nails should be kept cut very short, as to softness of skin on the soles I can say nothing from experience, as my feet never blister. Liniment of soap and whisky is recommended to harden them. In how far it is efficacious I know not. Glencoe has been described as the most tremendous pass in the highlands. It may be so, but I cannot prevail upon myself to think a great deal of it. Rugged it is indeed and grand, but it wants gloominess to give effect to its grandeur. The predominating colours are of the lighter kinds, gray or light blue and green. The very lake at the base of the great rock is light owing probably to the nature of its bottom which most likely is gravel, for there is little soil in the valley; and the rock itself, even though of the astonishing height of upwards of two thousand feet, wants the grandeur of simplicity or unity. For instead of appearing one vast mass, it resembles a great number of perpendicular rocks of no great height, rising behind each other, with the intervention of a steep slope of gray stones and gravel. Very different is the effect produced by a mass of rock which combines unity with grandeur. Such for example, as the noble mass of Stron Ulladil in the island of Harris, many of the cliffs in the Isles of Barray, several of the rocks of the Cullin mountains in Skye, the tremendous capes on the west side of the same island, and even the precipices of Ben Nevis, though these last are rather too much fissured and separated by chasms. Of all the tremendous scenes which I have seen, and not a few have come under my observation none equals that of Scavig in the bosom of the Callin mountains in the Isle of Mist. This glorious scene I therefore recommend to the contemplation of such of my readers as have a due attachment to the sublime, and if their enthusiasm be not so great as to carry them to the Isle of Skye, let them at least read the description of the scene in that tolerable sort of a poem of Wattie Scott, the scribbler entitled 'The Lord of the Isles'. After all I must say that none of these scenes produced astonishment. When I get among them I feel quite in my own element, just 'like a fish in water' (Goethe). There is an image in my mind however, which almost makes amend for the deficiency of satisfaction in regard to this particular. It is Hecla, vast, majestic, terrific Hecla. I see his tremendous black rocks piercing the clouds. I hear the roar of a thousand thunders, I feel the solid rock on which I stand tremble as the giant shakes his mighty frame. I see the dreadful, glorious eruption which illumines the dark isle of the north, and casts its dreary splendour over the frozen ocean. Clouds of black smoke roll around, the ground covered thick with cinders and ashes. I participate in the mute terror of the inhabitants of the earth, I adore the aweful majesty of that being who weighed the earth in a balance, and measure the waters in the palm of his hand. The birds which occurred today were Hedge Sparrow, Yellow-hammer, Rook, Raven, Pied Wagtail, Heron, Dipper, an eagle, and three species of hawk. I left Tyndrum on Monday after breakfast. Near the house and on the verge of the county I observed a post stuck up with the following notice 'Vagrants entering the county or found within the county of Perth will be apprehended and prosecuted as the law directs.' My remarks upon this must be deferred and I hasten to patch up my story. Near Tyndrum is a lead mine on the side of a hill. It has not been wrought there six years, and I did not in consequence visit it. For about eight miles I passed through a long dark valley, which was destitute of wood. At length a few trees appeared along the sides of the mountain, and soon after I came to the termination of the pass. The country became more open to the southwest. In the west the summits of Cruachan attracted my attention, and on emerging fairly from the pass a very beautiful scene presented. In the foreground I had a rough declivity covered by heath and bracken, and diversified with little round hills. The middle ground consisted of a valley, bounded on the north by a pretty steep hill, on the south by a gentle acclivity terminating in high heathy ground, at the distance of about two miles. Through the middle of this valley winded a river, which disappeared at intervals among the trees and brushwood which covered its banks. The valley extended toward Cruachan for about five or six miles, and was in its whole course occupied with cornfield and pasture ground. Houses and huts appeared here and there, and in one place the spire of a church. At the farther extremity of this valley were glimpses of a lake with a large castle on its banks. Beyond this, constituting the distant part of the scene, appeared the majestic Cruachan, rising in broken ridges to the clouds. The sky was clear and the sun shone bright, but a thin blue vapour shaded the distant part of the scene, and the dark shadows from the ridge of Cruachan gave a foreboding to its majestic form. This mountain, the highest in Argyll, is situated at the eastern extremity of Loch Awe, one of the largest lakes in Scotland, and on the confines of a broken plain stretching toward the sea. To me, who had just emerged from among the central mountains it did not appear very magnificent. I thought it a beautiful mountain however. The road led through the valley mentioned, which is called Glen Urchy, and which satisfied my expectations, to the eastern extremity of Loch-Awe. The ruinous castle which I had seen, I now found situated on a peninsula. It is named Kilchurn, in the Gaelic Caol-chiurn. Proceeding along the southern banks of the lake, I was often delighted with the beautiful scenes which presented. Several little tufted islands were seen and the sides of the lake were well wooded. In the evening I reached Cladich, a small village about six miles from the head of the lake, where I resolved to stay, as I had been thinking of devoting a day to the drawing of this beautiful scene. Taken at that time of day the scene would have been this. Thick woods of hazel, oak and birch, with cornfields and pasture in the foreground. Beyond this a portion of a lake several miles in extent, in which appeared several groups of very beautiful wooded islands. The background, a vast mountain divided near the summit into two by a rocky chasm, thickly wooded along its base which formed the distal margin of the lake, and diversified along its surface with little heights and shadowy vallies. The sun, about to set, shed a purplish lustre over the mountain, and produced an agreeable effect by the long shadows which it threw on the eminences. In one part in the extreme distance were mountains of great height, stretching far beyond Cruachan. I looked in vain for the blue and purple shades which ordinary painters dash most profusely even over the foreground of their scenes. The distant mountains were tinged with blue, and the shades of Cruachan had a purplish appearance. A thin bluish vapour also hung before distant objects, but blue and purple were by no means the predominant colours. Those who evade this error are apt to fall into another. They make their colouring too vivid. With water colours it is impossible in my opinion to imitate the blue vapour which produces the indistinctness or obscurity of distant objects, but a tolerable substitute may be formed by gradually diminishing the brightness of the colours and adding under certain circumstances blue or purple to them. It is wrong too in my estimation to paint landscapes by broad dashes, and with large pencils. Let anyone compare a landscape done in this way and an actual scene seen through the camera obscura, and he will easily perceive the great difference. In diminishing an object we ought to render the strokes finer, and the blending of colours less perceptible, and if with the greatest accuracy and minuteness no painter could make a perfect representation of a large object, such as a rock, or tree, or part of them drawn of the natural size, how can it be thought that with less accuracy he can make a good miniature resemblance of them? If I were to be a painter by profession, my aim would be to copy nature with the scrupulous, yea, even servile attention; instead of displaying a genius that scorned control by a masterly dash which would produce the likeness of nothing on earth. When I came to Cladich I looked for an Inn, but in vain. However I espied above the door of a small hut, the figure of a gill stoup and a glass. On approaching this mansion, I met the good woman who informed me after some grunting indicative of discontent that perhaps I might get accommodations. So I entered and drank a small quantity of birch water (see etymology of whisky). I then ordered supper and went for a walk. The night passed heavily, for I lay in a coarse bed, prevented from sleeping by the groans of a cow, heifer, stot, or stirk. I could not distinguish which, that lay on the other side of a partition that separated my bedroom from that of the cattle. It was about ten when I rose today. I found that the mountain was by far too near and too little seen of the lake to make a good landscape. So after breakfasting on bread and milk, I continued my journey. Travelling southward I passed over a dreary district in which Common Ling and Common Heather predominated. When I had advanced four miles I found that I was about to enter a wooded valley, and bethought me of noting the plants which should occur till I reached Inverary which I knew was five miles distant. As I advanced the woods increased till in the lower part of the valley I found myself in a forest of which the principal part consisted of exotic trees. Here I fell in with a lame woman seated in a chair fixed to a hand barrow, together with a man who appeared to be her husband and a boy. The woman desired me to carry her to a house at the distance of nearly a quarter of a mile. It is too far off said I. However I thought I might even do a worse action, and so with the assistance of the man carried her to the place mentioned. The usual "May God in heaven reward you" was of course applied as a recompense accompanied however with an "as I hope He will", which very plainly intimated that doubts were entertained regarding the accomplishment of the wish. Poor fool! thought I, if God rewarded every action of this kind, it would be an easy matter to purchase reward enough. The presumption of these creatures is amusing if not rather deplorable. If one gives them sixpence, or a shilling, or any sum above a halfpenny, they are very profuse of their blessings, as if they had the power of dealing out the favour of the Deity to whom they chose. I maintain that the blessings and cursings of any man or of all men are to be deemed in themselves of no importance, and that one need no more expect good from the blessings of the poor even though virtuous, than he need apprehend evil from the curses of the wicked or the good, for there is no distinction. If reward follows a good action, it is not the wish of any human being that can procure it; nor can we for a moment harbour the supposition that the Deity will bestow or withhold his favour according to the caprice of any frail child of the dust. The fuss of pastoral blessing so solemnly, rather so hypocritically solemnly bestowed upon congregations appears to me very absurd, as do many other things of their kind. But my candle is almost done, and I must leave my journal.

Luss, on Loch-lomond, Wednesday evening, 22nd September

It was a practice with me in former times when on my travels to drink upon certain occasions to the health of my friends and associates, and I have not forgot it. My readers will remember that I drank on a cold morning after having lain out all night by the side of a stone in a mountain glen, two glasses of pure aqua fortuna taken from the sources of the Dee to the health of four ladies, with two of whom I have the felicity of being intimately acquainted, and to the other two I have the honour of being partially known. Intimately acquainted, said I, yes, my remembrance is interwoven with the fibres of their hearts, and theirs with those of mine. It is my intention therefore, now that I am comfortably seated, by a nice little mahogany table, with two candles burning before me, in a very neat apartment in an excellent inn in the village of Luss on the banks of Lochlomond in Dumbartonshire to accompany with the exhilarating gustation of an indefinite number of glasses of 'spiritus frumenti cum aqua' the remembrance of a certain number of ladies. The ladies whose health I drank at the source of the Dee come first in order, and as to the rest I shan't tell names - no, that I won't - Jessy MacDonald, Mary MacDonald, Jessy Grant, Margaret Macleod, Jessy Simson, Helen MacCaskill, Helen MacFarlane, Mary MacKenzie. Odds-boddikins! I am in the isles now. Here the dear creatures, one and all, and lastly Kerry, and at the very end Jessy. But I must be serious though, so good-night my dear little angels.

It was nearly three o'clock when I reached Inverary yesterday. I felt delighted with the beauty of the scenes which presented there. However difficult it may be to awaken in me the sensations connected with the sublime or aweful, I am very susceptible of those attached to the beautiful, and here, it was impossible to turn in any direction which did not present beauties of no ordinary kind. I was on the northern bank of Loch Fyne, a very beautiful saltwater lake, about two miles in breadth and here of indefinite length, for at both extremities it appeared passing beyond the hills out of view. On the same side and at hand were the Castle of Inverary situated on a green plain and surrounded by lofty trees and the pleasure grounds in its vicinity consisting of lawns, forests, and hills covered with hanging groves. On the opposite side was a gentle acclivity, rising to a considerable height. Down the lake hills were seen on both sides having their sides wooded, and diversified with cornfields. Toward the head of the lake lofty mountains towered in the distance above the nearer hills which bore the same character as those in the opposite direction. The Castle is a very beautiful square building with circular towers at the angles. It is built of micaceous schists, and is in consequence of a light green colour, peculiarly beautiful, as neither having the glare of white granite, nor the gloom which sandstone assumes after a long exposure to the air. The town of Inverary, though a royal borough and the head town of the county looks almost like a set of offices belonging to the castle. After eating a very hearty dinner I proceeded on my journey, following the road to Dumbarton which passes along the margin of Loch Fyne. In the dusk I found myself at the head of the lake and soon after reached the Inn of Cairndow-dow on the south side, where I staid last night. Today I set out about nine, and ascended a mountain glen for some miles till I came to an emminence on the side of a lofty mountain. Before this I passed along the banks of an alpine lake in which I saw the black rocks of the mountain beautifully reflected. I stood for some time admiring the phenomenon, and confirmed the truth of an observation which I had made on a former occasion, that the images are reflected in right lines from the object to the eye, observing the law of reflection that the ray passes off from the surface at the same angle at which it touches it.

Thursday morning. When I had attained the extremity of this mountain glen I came upon another which winded downward between very rugged mountains. At its commencement, and on an elevated spot commanding an extensive prospect, I found a semicircular seat of turf, and near it a large stone with the following inscription REST AND BE THANKFUL 1748 Repaired by the XXIII Regt, 1768. As I felt no inclination to render my conduct conformable to the sage counsel of this sapient stone, I proceeded down the glen. I knew that the celebrated Glen Croe was in my course, and was looking out for terrific mountains, but saw none. Those which bounded the valley were indeed very rugged, and the rocks were black but they did not excite any extraordinary emotions. I sat down for a few minutes by the side of a milestone in this valley to discover by my little itinerary where I was, and what I might expect. By it I found that I had passed through the greater part of Glen Croe, and was near its mouth. It was described as 'an awful vale where all around is terrible'. I looked up to the mountains, but saw nothing very wonderful, so I burst into a fit of derisive laughter - Ha, ha, ha, ha, said I aloud, so this is Glencroe, the terrible Glencroe! Soon after I got a glimpse of Loch Long and seeing a sort of Inn by the road entered it, and ordered breakfast. In the meantime I repaired to a torrent which ran down the valley, and washed from head to foot. After breakfasting I passed on, and came to the banks of Loch Long, a saltwater lake. The scenery upon it was more in the highland style than that on Loch Fyne. Lofty mountains on both sides, with rapid slopes, wooded at their bases, and having a few patches of cornland here and there. At the head of the loch there was some fine scenery. This is the district of Arrochar, the ancient country of the MacFarlanes, a warlike but not very numerous tribe. By a dyke near the 26th milestone from Dumbarton, and close upon a bridge at the head of the lake I found a plant which I had not seen before, the Great Bindweed. It was still in flower and grew in considerable quantity. Before this time I had got a glimpse of Benlomond between the mountains and soon after entered a pass from which I saw it straight before me, and quite at hand. After walking about a mile in a wooded valley I came to Tarbert on the banks of Loch-lomond. Tarbert is a name applied in the Gaelic to a neck of land or isthmus between two pieces of water. Thus there is a Tarbert isthmus in the Islands of Harris and Cannay, another joining Cantyre to Argyle, another here between Loch-ling and Lochlomond. The weather was rather gloomy all day but there was no rain. I proceeded southwards along the western shores of the lake. Its surface was smooth as a mirror and reflected very distinctly the surrounding objects. I stood for some time admiring this beautiful phenomenon. The north end of the lake is narrow and bounded by very rugged mountains whose summits were at that time involved in mist. Here I saw a landscape in which blue and purple predominated. A blue vapour floated before the distant objects and though the green and dusky hues of the mountains were distinctly visible, yet in their reflected images, blue alone was to be seen, of a beautiful, clear, almost transparent softness, which it would be impossible to imitate. The gradual fading of colour dependent upon distance was much more palpably marked in the reflections than in the objects themselves. This was most beautifully displayed in the distant mountains on the lake, the nearest of which were reflected of a deep or bright, and the most distant of a pale blue. The colours of near objects were reflected without much alteration. The dark shades of the mountain rocks were rendered darker, but the lighter shades, such as green and yellow did not suffer any perceptible alteration, only that the objects were less distinct in the reflected image than in the original. As I was standing opposite Benlomond, making these observations, I heard a thundering sound in the north, and looking about saw a steam boat approaching. I could scarcely refrain from laughing at the incongruity of a steam engine puffing away on a highland lake. It soon after passed me and in less than an hour was out of sight. It completely destroyed my beautiful reflections, and for several miles farther I found the lake considerably agitated by it, with the wavelets dashing against the pebbly shores. "What an unnatural jumble is produced in this beautiful lake by that machine" grunted I aloud, with irritated feelings. When I had passed Benlomond which is on the eastern shore of the lake, and on which I had been in 1816, and proceeded a few miles farther, the lake widened and a beautiful scene presented. Beyond the lake I saw a flat or at least low country, and now feel the anticipated pleasure arising from novelty, for I began to tire of mountains and glens, rocks and torrents, and wished again to visit the haunts of men. The sides of the mountains along the lake are well wooded, and in some places the trees are of considerable size, though in general, as in almost all highland scenery they approach to the nature of brushwood. Oak is the most numerous species, but here is by no means monarch of the wood, being far overtopped by the more beautiful ash. Of Fir, I saw none. Indigenous fir is now almost extinct in the highlands. There are some forests of it in the upper part of Aberdeenshire, on Loch Maree in Ross-shire, and in a few other places. But its localities are now becoming so rare that in a short time they will require particular mention. There is no other species of Fir indigenous in Scotland. In Braemar I saw the Norway Fir, but it appeared to be planted, and the Larch everybody knows to be a foreigner. When I came to this expanded part of the lake, I found cultivated fields more frequent. The lake resumed its tranquillity, the evening was still and mild, and the Redbreast warbled his cheerful notes on the bushes which skirted the road. In the dusk I arrived at Luss, a village situated on the banks of the lake, shaded with trees, and surrounded by lofty mountains.

Dumbarton

It was about half past four this evening when I left the Inn of Luss. The writing of my notes of yesterday, and other circumstances had prevented me from getting away sooner. I thought proper to wait dinner and while it was preparing amused me with reading the inscriptions on the walls. Some of them, as is usual in such cases, were of a nature which prevented me from transcribing them. As this place is the resort of idlers of all descriptions from the hare-brained hunter after the picturesque to the vulgar city apprentice, these inscriptions were numerous and highly diversified. I thought that one might gather amusement and under certain circumstances even instruction, from the walls of an inn. I thought also that I might contribute to the amusement of my readers by laying before them a few of the most select of these extemporaneous ebullitions of Scottish humour, so here they are.

> Oh! cruel was the morning that was so very dull
> And cruel were the horses that would not faster pull
> Cruel was the weather that was so very wet
> And cruel was Benlomond to which we could not get

> Oh! cruel were the winds that blew so very high
> And cruel were the boats that could not with us ply

> a cruel abortive attempt (in another hand)

> He who goes to be, and goes to be sober
> Lives like the leaves and dies in October
> But he who goes to bed, and goes to bed mellow
> Lives as he ought to do, and dies an honest fellow

> When here we did arrive at last
> the day was dark and foggy-o
> so down to rest ourselves we cast
> and took a wee drap groggie-o

Five young ladies, rank highlanders

Sweet peaceful glen I dearly love
Thy streams and fertile plains
Thy hills, thy dales, thy all, except
Thy never-ending rains

rather good and true (13th June 1819)

Ah! woe is me! my tender heart
Is split by Cupid's fatal dart
    Send it to a tinsmith
Ah! woe is me! it was a sad disaster
When you became a poetaster

You'll ask who am I
Among the girls a nailer
A blade of spirit high
Though but a simple - tailor

A very good song
And very well sung
Jolly companions
One and all

While searching among these inscriptions, I fell upon a couplet written in a character which I thought I recognised as the handwriting of Mr Cockerill. Very different from the sensations which the other pieces excited were those which I experienced on reading this

    Oh! What can sanctify the joys of home
    Like Hope's gay glance from ocean's gleaming foam.

Immortal Byron, said I, if this is not thine, I know not whose it is. It struck the chord to which my heart had accorded for seven days. My reflections however must be deferred. There is not, and has not been, in my estimation, a poet equal to Byron. The third canto of his Childe Harold rises proudly pre-eminent above all the productions of poetic genius, as his favourite Mount Blanc overtops the European hills. To the poetical effusions on the walls of this apartment I deemed it meet and becoming to add the following which I had composed last night as fast as my fingers could guide the pen in committing it to a leaf of my memorandum book. It was composed after the health-drinking at an interlude before my beginning to write my notes. It displays a vast degree of genius, and like its author is irregular in the measure.

> Light-heel'd levity be gone
> And leave me all alone
> For I am going to speak of mountains,
> Forest, rocks, and fountains,
> Bubbling rill, and roaring torrent;
> Awe-struck mind, and visage horrent.
> First of all, Benlomond high -
> On his top Oh! let me die
> or at least be buried
> Where my ghost may wander
> Amid clouds and thunder
> By the tempest hurried
> Then Glencroe where Saxons go
> To view the black sublime
> Which Heaven in mercy to their clime
> Refus'd to grant them so.
> O Jupiter now hear my prayer
> 'Dead or alive let me but be renown'd'
> My throne Ben-nevis in mid-air
> There let me sit and laugh
> With Ossian, Fingal, Gaul, and Oscar
> From scallop shells to quaff

Sweet uisge-beath - the Highland nectar
And Terrify at times the world
With sheets of snow and black rocks surl'd
From our high seat.
It is full meet
That I should wake the lyre
Then Harp of Ossian sound, Oh sound
Awake the strains, the living fire
That make the mountain-gael to bound
With active limb and gleesome face
The ball-room barn, or kiln to pace,
While many a beauteous nymph sits there
With greasy face and feet all bare
And gaping mouth, and staring eyes
And gnomon pointing to the skies -
Ye Gods! I am on fire
Burning with poetic ire
And if in Lomond's crystal wave
'My youthful limbs I were to lave'
I'm very sure 't would raise a fuss
Aye - just as sure as I'm in Luss

After paying my bill which I found amounted to a pretty round sum I continued my journey. For nearly two miles I passed along the lake which here was studded thick with beautiful wooded islands, some of which were pretty large. The road then left the banks of the lake, and passed through extensive woods, till about four miles from Luss when I again came upon it. The evening was calm and serene. The surface of the lake was perfectly smooth, a blue transparent vapour hung before the distant objects - the little Robin warbled his enlivening notes on the hawthorn bushes which edged the road. When I had reached the lower extremity of the lake the sombre shades of evening began to involve the distant landscape in obscurity, and to blend the majestic Benlomond with the surrounding clouds. On the Rowan trees by the road I observed the Fieldfare, and the Thrush or perhaps the Redwing picking the berries. The road after this became hemmed in with hedges, trees, and dykes, so that I could see but little around me. And when I had reached the eight milestone from Luss night fell. Of the surrounding scenery I saw nothing after this, only I learned by the trees, the cornfields, the houses, and the hum of men, that I was passing through a fertile and populous district. A little more than two miles from this place I passed a large village at the nearer end of which I saw the monument of Smollet who has so beautifully described the scenery of this valley in his elegant ode to Leven Water. During the rest of my course I heard the voices and the footsteps of men. Of course I could not consider myself as solitary, but in regard to personal safety I would much rather be in Glencroe at such an hour than in this place. One may travel over the highlands by night as well as by day. Robbery was scarcely ever heard of there, at least the mean sort of robbery to which I allude. But here in the vicinity of Glasgow, where the scum of the earth is raked together, it is not advisable for a single traveller to walk late, especially if unarmed as I am, for I have not even a sprig of shilelah*. However if a fellow were to fall foul of me, I think that, keeping of firearms, I would make good my ground. I had even determined to proceed to Glasgow tonight, but when I got here I found myself so tired that I could not keep my resolution, the bells were striking eight o'clock when I reached the skirts of the town. It was not without pleasure, that from the bridge which crosses the Leven I surveyed the dark shades of the town with its glimmering lights, and heard the well-known hum of the 'ignobile volgus' and the more pleasing sounds of a flute from the opposite side of the river. I have now fairly emerged from my beloved mountains, and tomorrow will open my eyes upon Lowland scenery and Saxon faces.

The shores of Lochlomond appear to furnish good ground for the botanist. Near Luss I observed the Floating Bur-reed and either the White or Yellow Water-lily, or both. Here I also found the Three-cleft Bur-marigold and soon after in a marshy piece of ground the Nodding Bur-marigold, which I have just examined. Besides these I have examined the Common Oak and Chestnut Tree, from specimens brought with me. The latter however was not indigenous there.

Glasgow

Yesterday the shades of night hid from my view a beautiful lake, covered with wooded islands, apparently bounded in the distance by a majestic mountain.

* This is presumably a reference to the more typically Irish cudgel, the shillelagh.

Today the first objects which I beheld were a city, a vast cultivated plain, a large navigated river, and an immense fortified mass of rock. After passing a restless night, I rose before eight o'clock and went out to look about me. The rock of Dumbarton attracted my notice and I proceeded to it without delay. A soldier accompanied me to its summit. Miss Porter makes too great by far about this rock and castle, and in truth in the whole of her Scottish Chiefs there is a great deal of bombast. Few authors know the advantages of simplicity of diction or are able to acquire it. The rock of Dumbarton is I believe far superior to those of Edinburgh, Stirling or Dunottar as a place of defence, because unlike them it rises abruptly from a level plain. It is split into two at the summit, and in the cleft are built barracks. The works are trifling, because the place requires very little assistance from art, being an almost complete natural fortress. In two places only may the works be approached, at the gate and by a rugged slope on the east side of the rock, at the top of which the wall is not high. In the guardroom I was shown the sword of Sir William Wallace. About nine I returned to the Inn, and breakfasted about ten. When on my way to the Castle I found two species of Mallow, the Common Mallow and the Musk Mallow, the latter of which was new to me. It was completely out of flower. Before eleven o'clock I left Dumbarton, and proceeded toward Glasgow. The road passed in the whole of this course along the Clyde, but at some distance from it. The country is fertile and well cultivated. There is abundance of wood also, and the fences are generally of hawthorn. Unlike the huts on Lochawe or Lochleven, the abodes of the peasantry are neat and comfortable. Every thing in short tended to impress the idea of civilisation. But the physical character of the inhabitants appeared to be at variance with the scenery. Countenances were seen every now and then with the horrid marks of urban vulgarity or rather of blackguardism, I know no word as applicable as this, urban vulgarity I say in opposition to rustic, though the term urban is commonly used in a very different sense, for they are widely different. The ignorance of the peasant may excite a smile and the uncouthness of his manners may afford subject of ridicule, but the diabolic depravity of the city blackguard however blended with awkward vulgarity, must excite pure horror and detestation. To the former one even feels kindness, and wish to overlook his little innocent blunders - but with the latter we have no sympathy. The very women in this district had a masculine air - rather their countenances expressed extreme coarseness of sentiment, and habitual impudence, or at least want of delicacy. And as to beauty, there was none of it. I have not seen a beautiful girl since I left Aberdeen, though I walked today over a great part of this city. I saw one handsome, but not beautiful young lady indeed yesterday, near Luss. The peculiar features of the highlanders have no connection with those expressions of depravity in the lowlanders. The former may sometimes appear savage, but the latter are diabolic. Of the different sorts of faces which attracted my attention here the most ridiculous were those of some dragoons which I met, whiskered and mystachioed from the chin to the ears. One of them in particular had very long red mystachioes which near the mouth assumed a whitish tinge, they looked of all things like the whiskers of an old red cat which had been licking cream. These blockheads think to render themselves formidable by leaving their beards uncut. I am much mistaken if an honest soberly decent man is not in a good cause worth two of such scarecrows. The British soldiery have always been noted for their plainness, and for their bravery, and I am apprehensive that when foppery is introduced among them, weakness and irresolution will accompany it. Perhaps I am mistaken, and perhaps when a fellow is 'bearded like the pard' 'Shakespeare' he assumes as a necessary consequence the ferocity of that animal. But after all ferocity is a far less valuable quality in a soldier than bravery, and bravery is inferior to fortitude - and true fortitude in my opinion can only be possessed by a good man conscious of his integrity, or by a bad man who is firmly persuaded that he is acting justly, it matters not which. It is not absolute virtue, but the consciousness of it, whether true or false, that inspires fortitude. Witness the conduct of the Covenanters, the Bramins, of the North American Indians etc. But how the profane blackguardish troopers can have either actual virtue, or its ideal conviction, is to me incomprehensible. Steam-boats appeared in abundance upon the Clyde today. The consideration of the effects of civilization is truly amazing. The room in which I am sitting is lighted by gas, as are the streets and most of the houses of this city. About Dumbarton the view is rather limited laterally by hills, but four miles from that place it becomes extensive over a flat country. I saw on the other side of the river the town of Paisley which I shall soon visit. Bye the bye, I have been in Glasgow before, and have sailed up the Clyde from the mouth of Lochfyne in Argyll. Yet all that I have seen today bore the character of novelty, even the rock of Dumbarton and

Glasgow itself. The country between this and Dumbarton is very rich in plants. I found several which I had not seen before, and I dare say might have augmented my list considerably if I had searched the country.

Inn of Ellieston Bridge, Renfrewshire

I rose about nine, breakfasted, and taking in my hand Smith's Compendium went out to search for the Botanic Garden, to see which I had gone to Glasgow. I walked through the streets for some time. The old red cat, or bearded dragoon, of yesterday met me. The streets were crowded. A considerable number of well formed males occurred. I did not see one sentimental face however, nor any in which the characters of genius or nobility were legible. All were keenly intent on purely terrestrial concerns and the ideas of all were associated with particular objects. The expression of intense thought, condensed into the scrutiny of abstract principles, cognizable in contraction and sharpening of the eyelids, accompanied with perpendicular wrinkles on the forehead, did not occur. Nor, in short did I see a noble face but one, and that one not belonging to a living wight, but forming the most interesting part of a statue, larger than life, of Sir John Moore, the hero of Corunna, a native of Glasgow. It is of bronze, and placed upon a pedestal of white granite from Aberdeen. This, bye the bye, makes it necessary for me to mention that Glasgow is entirely built of sandstone, or freestone, as it is commonly called. Scotland is not the land of statues and columns. I was therefore pleased with the sight of this, and I found it far superior to what I had at first imagined it. The face and hair are admirably done, and indeed the whole, only I was not pleased with the want of energy in the hands. The form and habitual position, or rather degree of contraction of the hands express a great deal. Any person may convince himself of this by a week's observation. The usual tapering of the fingers and the feeble delicacy of the whole hand, seen in prints by British artists, is very absurd and very intolerable. Short, thick fingers only can be attached to one particular kind of frame, long and delicate to another, and so on. Female fingers only taper - those of the male ought to be flattened at the points. The hands of this statue, though almost faultless in regard to form, wanted the expression of energy - so much regarding masculine beauty. The females which I met were far inferior to the males. To those who are pleased with physical beauty I would recommend the town of

Perth. There on a fine day it is impossible to proceed a hundred yards on the streets without meeting figures and faces which might bring to the mind the descriptions of the Ionian Isles. The causes of this I know not! Next to Perth, of the Scottish towns, is Aberdeen, and next to it, Edinburgh. The women of Glasgow are almost frightful. On enquiring in a bookseller's shop the situation of the Botanic Garden, I found that it lay to the west of Glasgow, and there, a little beyond Anderston, one of the suburbs, I found it. At the Gate I met a man who informed me that without recommendation from one of the subscribers or proprietors I could not gain admittance. He asked if I was a gardener, I answered of course, that I was not, but that I was a student of Natural History, at that time, travelling. On my telling him, in answer to one of his questions, that I came from Aberdeen, he said he would acquaint his master - so he did, and I was admitted. In the greenhouse I found the Superintendent, who was very polite, and very attentive, and extremely sorry that he could not accompany me through the hothouse garden. However full liberty was granted me to view the whole, and I proceeded leisurely to take a superficial scrutiny of the place.

Sunday morning.

The Botanic Garden of Glasgow was instituted in 1817. It is not therefore yet stocked, but upwards of seven thousand species have been collected, an immense number for the short space of two years. It occupies a space of nearly eight English acres. At one corner is a house of two flats, the lower occupied by the gardener, the upper intended for a lecture room, and for the meetings of the directors. Nearly in the centre are the hothouses, greenhouse, and shades for the utensils. In front of the hothouse is a pond for the aquatic plants, and near it a heap of rough stones with walks over it for alpine and rupestrine plants. The walks are all flexuous excepting four parallel with the walls. In one division the plants are arranged according to the Linnaean system and labelled. In the rest of the garden they are placed without order. The smallness of the walks, and the want of large trees give it a bare, inelegant, disagreeable appearance. And as it was intended as much for a pleasure garden, as for a botanic one, I think it ought to have been laid out in a very different manner. It is the joint property of a number of subscribers. The Faculty of the College contributed two thousand pounds, and have the right of appointing the directors from their own body. The

Professor of Botany delivers a course of Lectures in the garden annually. While looking among the plants I examined by my Compendium the following species, some of which I had known before, though I had not minutely inspected them. They were Common Flowering Rush, Greater Spear-wort. Common Hart's-tongue, Pale Mountain Polypody, Dwarf Mallow, and Common Marsh-mallow.

I returned about two o'clock. At this time it rained heavily. I had formed a scheme of going to see the Hunterian Museum, and after that of proceeding to the theatre, but I began to feel impatient and after some hesitation packed up my portables and sallied out. Crossing the Clyde by the New Bridge, I soon gained the Paisley road and proceeded on my journey. It was about half past three when I left Glasgow, and about half past five I entered Paisley, the distance being seven miles. There have been some riots of late in Glasgow and Paisley and I was informed that it would be extremely dangerous to travel at night. However my impatience would not be overcome, and I proceeded. In the dusk I passed two fellows quarrelling on the road, and afterwards several squads of blackguardish men. One of them was shouting "Damnation - good bread and bear scones" was what he wanted. However no person molested me and at eight o'clock I arrived here. Both my wrists and one cheek are swelled enormously from the bites of bugs which I got in Glasgow. I had thought the animals were to be dreaded only in old houses, but even in the Inn at Luss on Lochlomond, I got a bite on the temple. The bite of a bug, though to some people very trifling, is to me a serious disaster, for my skin is so irritable that the least cut or scratch always festers. The tumour on my cheek was last night as large as a hen's egg, and today it has a scab upon it from serious effusion. Those upon my wrist and two upon my right arm were nearly as large, and have small blisters on the top. A bite which I got on the wrist three years ago, suppurated and was a month in healing, and its mark remains to this hour. Today the weather is fine. It is now ten o'clock and I must be off.

Ayr, Monday morning, 8 o'clock, 27th September 1819

Yesterday I passed through a beautiful and fertile country. Soon after leaving Bridge of Ellieston I passed the lake and town of Lochwhinnoch, and three miles farther on entered the town of Beith. Between Beith and Kilwinning some fine specimens of crystalline quartz from a heap of limestone which lay beside the road. Here also I obtained my first view of the Western Ocean, and saluted Ailsa by a halloo. The scenery now improved greatly. To the south I saw a wide extended county bounded by hills and washed by the ocean. To the west the Isle of Arran and Cantyre. Between Kilwinning and Irvine I went off the highway, and found myself obliged to ford a river which reached as high as my waistcoat. In the dusk, or rather about sunset, I entered the town of Irvine situated near the sea. On the South side of it I found links exactly similar to those which extend along the Copts from Aberdeen to Newburgh. I left the highway and proceeded along these links for several miles. They were occupied with rabbits of which I saw several hundreds. Bye the bye I also saw a hare today. The only wild Quadrupeds then which have occurred since I left Aberdeen were the mole, red deer, mountain hare, and brown hare. Here I also found and examined the Field Scabious. I then regained the highway. The moon and stars shone bright, and there was an agreeable keenness in the air. I felt therefore very cheerful, and perfectly free from apprehension of anything. About halfway between Irvine and Ayr I fell in with a man, who walked upwards of a mile with me. I enquired of him concerning Dr John Macleod with whom Mr MacLachlan is at present on a visit. He informed me that his house was not more than two miles distant from the place in which we were, that he was very much disliked by his parishioners, and that a person answering to the description of Mr MacLachlan was with him. I regretted that I had not stayed at Irvine in order to see Mr MacLachlan today. I reached Ayr at nine o'clock, and after searching nearly half an hour found a bed. But it had been better for me that I had slept by a hedge, for I am almost completely covered with tumours and vesications produced by the bites of bugs. I didn't sleep through the night, and today got up about six, and visited the Briggs O' Ayr. When I returned I thought it proper to take some stimulus, this however increased my malady. I am at present feverish in a high degree, that is I have a great thirst. General heat, rapid pulse, headache, and nausea. My left eye is nearly closed, and there is a great tumour upon the cheek which suffered in Glasgow. How gladly would I have exchanged my bed of last night with the couch of grass on the side of Cairngorm. The weather is bad today too. I must change my lodgings however.

Kirk Alloway, Monday. Noon.

Here I am in a window of the far famed Kirkalloway, but not in the 'winnoch buner in the east' where 'sat auld Nick' for that is placed beyond my reach by a wall built across the Church to preserve from profanation the dust of a 'parcel of precious Lairds of Doonside'. I am now much better than I was three hours ago. The blast of ocean has revived me. I left Ayr about ten, and wandered about for some time in search of this place, till at length about a quarter of an hour ago I found it. Not far from this is the cottage in which Burns was born. It is now converted into a 'publick house' as it is called. I entered it and got a half-mutchkin of the favourite potation of the unfortunate bard. I kneeled down upon the floor with my hat off. "Immortal Burns" said I aloud, "here on my knees I do homage to thy genius" and pouring the liquor on the floor added "and pour forth this libation - to thy memory". Poor fellow! there never was a genius upon earth whose memory is dearer to my heart. He holds the same place in my estimation as Linnaeus and Sterne. Let others make their pilgrimage to the shrines of hypocritical saints and deluded bigots; I will visit the scenes consecrated to the memory of the Children of Nature. My God is the father of all mankind. His favour and protection are not confined to 'a chosen people'. His temple is universal nature. His true worshippers are those whose hearts are warm with the glow of benevolence. Big drops are trickling down my cheeks - I know not why - I cannot scrutinize my feelings. The spirit of departed years speaks to my soul, and the meteor phantoms of futurity hover around. My soul is sad. When will the light of heaven flash through the murky clouds of ignorance and doubt that have enveloped it?

Monday evening.

The roar of waters is around me. I am now upon the seashore. The sun has set behind Cantyre. The horizon is edged with dusky clouds. Before me is the rock of Ailsa rising alone from the ocean, in the northwest is the isle of Arran with its lofty mountains, in the west the dimly distinguished hills of Cantyre. I am still unwell but not melancholy. The sight of the glorious ocean has restored my serenity. How I am to be lodged tonight I know not. The nearest town is upwards of five miles distant, and I am scarcely able to move. However I shall proceed.

Girvan, Ayrshire, Tuesday 28th September

It is necessary for me to begin my story of yesterday anew. About ten o'clock I left Ayr, and proceeded along a road which passed by the sea shore. About a mile from the town, as I was looking at the Isle of Arran, I was accosted by a man with "your servant, Sir". I did not like the sound of his voice and did not turn about. The salutation was repeated however, and on turning about I beheld one of the most rascal visages I had seen for some time. "How do you do Sir?" asked the fellow in a low muttering tone. "Pretty well" answered I in a repressing one. "Have you travelled far?" "Not very far". "Do you know if there be any vessels in Ayr for Ireland?" "I don't know". He still manifested no disposition to depart, and stood beside with his face half averted. "Good morning, friend" said I to myself, and proceeded. Soon after I came upon the river Doon, but found that I had taken the wrong road to Burn's Cottage. So I passed up a long avenue by the river, and at length found the cottage. From it I proceeded to Kirk Alloway which was not far off, and on the north bank of Doon. As one part of it was shut up by an iron door and a wall built across the church I was obliged to get upon the top of the wall to get a view of it. I then descended and wrote a little into my journal, merely for the sake of the locality. I looked for plants to take with me, but found none worth preserving excepting two or three specimens of Wall-rue Spleenwort which grew upon the walls. These I added to my collection and proceeded. I then crossed Doon by a bridge placed a little below that on which Meg lost her tail. The country soon after began to assume a different aspect. Hitherto it had been plain, or rather a gentle slope from gentle hills of no great elevation. But when I reached Maybole, a small town situated out of view of the sea, at the distance of eight miles from Ayr, I found the countryside a different nature. To the south and east, at a considerable distance, were pretty high hills, apparently heathy on their summits. Between these and the town were gentle emminences and depressions. There were fewer trees also, but hawthorn was still used for fences. At Maybole I ate some bread, my headache was by this time intense. About a mile and a half beyond Maybole I passed the ruins of a Cathedral and Castle. A woman of whom I enquired told me they were called Crossregal. Farther on I bathed my right arm in a streamlet. It was stiff and painful and swelled from the fingers to the shoulder. Near the elbow I found it considerably upwards of two inches larger in circumference than the other which had escaped.

Some miles farther on I came upon the sea about sunset. There is such an idea of liberty always associated in my mind with the view of the ocean that the sight of it in the present case revived me much. I was pleased also with the sight of two or three Solan Geese (Gannet) who were coasting. The rock of Ailsa appeared just opposite, and about eighteen miles distant. It reminded me of the Isles of Hirt as seen from the mountains of Harris. The moon shone in the south, and soon after the stars appeared. I determined to proceed, for a cool breeze from the south allayed the burning heat of my face and dispelled my headache. About four miles farther I attempted to ascend a half formed stack of corn but did not succeed, so I thought I should even go to Girvan for a bed. I proceeded accordingly, soon after crossed Girvan water, and arrived here at eight o'clock. My landlady, by way of kindness, sat at table with me, and made my tea. I proposed several questions to her relative to the country which she answered.

Last night as I was entering Girvan I saw three glorious flashes of lightning. It rained some through the night, but today the weather is very fine. I slept till nine o'clock in a good bed, and am now quite well and fresh. Only the swelling has not entirely subsided. For the mention of more particulars I have not time, as it is now twelve o'clock and I must proceed.

Ballintrae, Ayr-shire, Tuesday evening

About a quarter after twelve I left Girvan. It is a large village, situated near the sea shore on a plain bounded at no great distance by hills. The aspect of the country I found was now completely changed. Scarcely any trees were to be seen, and the hawthorn hedges were short and unhealthy. The country was hilly, but a plain extended along the sea shore. Directly west of Girvan is the rock of Ailsa, nearly in the same direction is seen the Mull of Cantyre, in the north west the Isle of Arran, and in the west and south west the coast of Ireland. The part of Ayrshire over which I had passed abounds in limestone. Some of the houses were built of it, with facings of sandstone for the doors and windows. The abodes of the peasantry are neat, at least they look comfortable and cleanly. They are in general thatched, as slate is not found in the country. Coal is also found abundantly in Ayrshire. It is not there however of the best quality, being slaty and not caking like the Newcastle coal. The cows of Ayrshire are noted for the quantity of milk which they yield. My landlady of last night informed me that she had seen cows which gave sixteen or even eighteen Scotch pints in the day. They are in general large and clean-limbed. The universal colour is light red mixed more or less with white. Some are horned, others not. Dr Johnson, very gravely, and very confidently too, tells us that a hornless cow is a distinct species from a horned one. But the doctor, like many others, was meddling with things about which he knew nothing. Two miles from Girvan I observed a plant on the sea shore which I knew at first sight to be the Sea Eryngo. I compared its characters with those in my compendium and found that I was correct. The finding of this plant afforded a great deal of pleasure for it is rare in the north, and though I had been informed that it was to be found in North Uist, I did not find it there, and had not seen it before. At this place was beach composed of sand and pebbles mixed. The other plants which I observed upon it were Prickly Saltwort, Spreading Halbert-shaped Orache, Sea Reed, Sea Milkwort, and Hemlock Stork's-bill, and others not purely maritime. For two miles farther the road passed along the shore which was rocky but low. The plants which I observed in that space, besides those mentioned were Sea Campion, Buck's-horn Plantain, Sea Plantain, Common Scurvy-grass, White English Stonecrop, and Common Thrift. The Common Hemlock occurred by the road-side, but rarely. It is very rare on the road between this and Glasgow. The Burdock is common. Four miles from Girvan the road leaves the shore, and ascends a hill over the side of which it passes for about two miles. On this hill I observed a plant unknown to me. I readily found it to be the Common Flea-bane. The beautiful Grass of Parnassus occurred on this hill, but in Ayrshire it appears to be rare. After leaving this hill I came to a narrow plain extending for about a mile along the shore, covered with immense masses of rock resembling the ruins of a city of giants, and bounded on the land side by low hills. On this plain I saw a stone which marked the graves of two natives of Arran who had been wrecked there. At the south end of it I observed the Hare's-foot Trefoil, and Sea Radish growing along with Sea Eryngo among Sea Reed. This was seven miles from Girvan. Soon after the road left the shore and passed over some hills on which nothing remarkable occurred. Ten and a half miles from Girvan I came to a narrow plain which I saw stretching along the shore to Ballintrae, a distance of two miles and a half. This plain is about a quarter of a mile in breadth. In this space was an abundance of the Sea Reed for about a mile from the northern extremity, the rest was grassy.

There are fewer plants in flower than when I left Aberdeen, and the trees are beginning to fade. Here there are no trees, the land is hilly, but not very high. Sheep and cows are kept, and there is not much cultivated land. No heath however appears excepting on some of the hills in the interior. it is not absolutely wanting however by the road between this and Girvan, for I have seen specimens of Common Ling and Common Heath there, but they were extremely rare, and in no place did I see a square foot of heath.

The birds which I saw today were of the following species; Gannet, Common Gull, Pied Wagtail, Rook, Crow, Robin, Meadow Pipit, Shag, and Hedge Sparrow. The rook was seen in great flocks among the drift wave or sea plants upon the shore. I expected to find some sandpipers but saw none. The gannet was rarish. It is absurd to name this bird Pelecanus bassanus as if it were to be found only on the Bass Isle. Might it not with as great propriety be named P. ailsensis (after Aisla Craig) or P. hirtanus, (after St. Kilda). Specific names taken from countries are perfectly intolerable. The Genista angliea is very common in Scotland. The Ligusticum scoticum (Scottish Lovage) is found in England, the Pinguicula lusitanica (Pale Butterwort) in Scotland, the Trollius europaeus (Mountain Globeflower) in Asia and so forth.

Wherever I go I sniff the air to discover if there be bugs, just as the terrified reindeer pricks his ears to catch the distant buzz of the gadfly. They have a peculiar smell. Be it known to you, O' gentle reader, that I am about to deliver a short account of this interesting animal (the bed bug). It belongs to the Order Aptera of the Class Insecta of the Animal Kingdom. It is a small insect of a flat rounded figure, something like the ticks of sheep or dogs, without wings. It inhabits the seams and chinks in old wood, especially the wood of beds, hence its name Cimex lectuarius, or as one might say in English, the bed tick. During the day it lies concealed and does not venture out, but at night it makes predatory excursions among the bed clothes, and if a band of them happen to fall in with the soft skin of a 'fat fodgel wright' (Burns) woe, woe be to him, and woe, and scratching with nails, and torment, and gnashing of teeth. The rapidity of its motions enables it to escape detection with facility. Its bite is not accompanied with pain, at least with intense pain. Hence the sufferer cannot direct his digital forceps to the spot. Soon after the bite is inflicted the part feels itchy and painful, the rubbing which follows increases the malady, the part swells, and continues to rise for about fifteen or eighteen hours when it subsides, leaving a yellowed mark which continues for several days. Some people are much more severely affected by their bite than others, this being dependent on the delicacy of their skins. Some even feel very little inconvenience from them, while others, if the bites be extensive and continuous become seriously indisposed, and affected with febrile symptoms, or at least with a most tormenting and intolerable sensation. It continues its attacks all night, but when daylight appears it betakes itself to its crevices. From these seams and chinks they may be taken with pins, but they cannot be entirely destroyed in this way. The decoction of several plants destroys them, of tobacco for instance. Irish lime has the same effect, hence it is a common practice in districts where they abound to sprinkle the floors with it, as in Glasgow where among the poorer sort they are common. Several preparations of mercury also destroy it. It first found its way into Scotland sometime in the seventeenth century. It is not to be found in the more northern parts however. To the north of Inverness it is not known and to most of the Western isles it has not extended. Even in Aberdeen it is very rare, I have seen specimens however collected there.

I am at present in a very good Inn belonging to a namesake. He spells his name however in a very odd manner Macilwrath! It is proper enough in my judication to have an etymological discussion in the present case, and I like philological dissertation very much. Well then. The original is MacGill'o bhraith, which signifies son or descendant of the lad of the hillside or upper country. The Gil o bhraith himself was probably some freebooter, and a smart fellow who lived in some inaccessible mansion in the upper part of a district in the highlands. Braith, in Scotch brae, is applied to such a part, for example Brae Mar, Brae Murray, Brae Rannoch, the Brae of Lochaber, of Loch Carron, and in general Braigh na duthcha, the Brae of the country is applied to the upper or inland part of any district. Now the son of this robber would of course be named Mac GilloBraith, Mac signifying son, his descendant retained the name. Agreeably to the common analogy the name should be rendered in English, MacGilvrae. I retain mine however as I got it from my daddy, for it is scarcely worth one's while to fall out with his name. But MacIlwraith is a most horrible distortion. I account for it thus. Some mean fellow of the clan emigrated and came among the lowlanders. He could not write of course, and knew not how his name was spelt. His English was bad, hence he pronounced his own name MacIlvrai, ai like the ae of the Greeks, or like the English word, aye. The letter v is that which by a highlander is commonly substituted in his pronunciation of an English word for w. Hence the lowlanders among whom the descendant of the robber came would very naturally spell the name in the first instance MacIlivrai. Now if it had remained MacIlvrai or Ilvrae or Ilvray, all had been well enough, but how the 'th' came to be added, I know not. The 'th' of the Saxons is a sound utterly unknown to the Gael. Hence the Highland student of the English language pronounces it t or d, thus 'throw away that nasty thing', he would pronounce it 'tro afuawy tat naisti ting'. The Lowlanders therefore among whom the Gael came might think that this was the case with his pronunciation of his name, and might add the th on that account. Be this as it may I care not a quarter of a farthing about the matter. My name according to analogy should be, as I have said, MacGilvrae, and the accent should be on the last syllable. But since the name is anglified the accent is placed with propriety on the second syllable. In the same way is pronounced anemone in English. But (as I have said) I shall retain MACGILLIVRAY for the present at least. Gentle reader, you may deem this a matter of no mighty consequence, but I would advise you to reflect that this paper is more mine than yours. Bye the bye I am much indebted to these readers, this is written for myself, their ideal existence accompanies me everywhere. There for instance is Dr A, and Mr B, Mrs C, and Miss D, and so on. The very ideal association of them makes me laugh at times, for they are very different in disposition and qualifications. To some of them this journal will yield instruction, to some amusement, to some it will be the subject of ridicule, and who the devil cares? I laugh at the idea of being ridiculed, or pitied, or despised. I feel a great deal more haughty and conceited when I am overlooked than when I am elevated beyond my station, and I have experienced both. By the way, as I have just been among Gaelic, I may add a few words still upon the subject. When the Lowlander or Englishman says that the Highlander is not well acquainted with the English language, often uses the feminine pronoun she for himself, he tells a falsehood. The case is this. In the Gaelic, as in the French, there are but two genders, the masculine and feminine. A Highlander learning English of course thinks that it has but two genders also. Hence he calls a stone she, the fire he, his arm and foot are feminine, his mouth and ears masculine. As to a neuter gender it never enters into his conception. But he does not conceive himself to be of the feminine gender nor his wife of the masculine. I never heard a highlander call himself she, and I have heard more bad English among them, than most of those who make the assertion whose foundation in truth I deny. His English is ridiculous because he adheres to the idiom of his native language, and uses only two genders. But he never uses any other pronoun to designate himself than I or me. Let who will deny this and I will undertake to prove him a liar from prejudice, or presumption, or folly, or obstinacy, or ignorance, or all. I have got a noble apartment in the house of my namesake, and have treated myself better than usual, and this entirely for the good of the house, as the saying is. And now that it is I dare say twelve o'clock, I shall finish my cogitations together with my toddy and drink a draught to the health of my friends. I have now got into my bedroom, and of course am not apprehensive that I will keep the maid too long out of her bed waiting to show me to mine. Bye the bye, it is an improper practice in inns to send a girl to show people to their beds, and very indecorous. I am not very sure what the reason of it is. Most men however, who are the principal visitors of inns, especially young men, like better to be shown to bed by a girl than a fellow, especially if she be good looking, and be it observed that in good inns the girl is generally so. In the parlour of this Inn there is a large mirror above the fireplace. It is a good idea, I protest, to give a fellow the satisfaction, as he is warming himself, of admiring his own precious person, and when I turn Innkeeper I shall place a mirror over every fireplace in my house. Farm-yards, dung-hills, cow-byres, and sheep-parks should be inspected by every traveller of taste, in case he might in future time become a farmer. Bye the bye, I saw on Lochlomond at the gate of some blockhead of fortune, a mountain ash, and near it an oak with their branches lopped off in the French cropped style. If they were mine I should level them to the dust. In the Highlands the gentry have very little taste. There is always something out of repair about the houses. The poorer people have no idea of the comfort of a good house, nor have they any notion of the sublime or the picturesque. Hence they would prefer a low flat country to their own because more fertile. When a Lowlander or Englishman speaks to them of the beauty of their rugged mountains, they do not comprehend him, shrug their shoulders, and say that they are grand, that is ugly and barren. Their attachment to their native country depends therefore more upon their friends than with localities, of this I am not sure however. A great number of circumstances must be considered in determining a case of this kind. Only a Highlander has more affection for his friends than a Lowlander.

Stranraer, Wigton-shire, Wednesday evening 29th September

After breakfasting in MacIlwrath's I proceeded on my journey. Ballintrae is a small village, composed of pretty good houses however, situated on the sea shore. About a quarter of a mile from it I crossed the Strichar which here falls into the sea. The exquisite simple and pathetic song of Burns, 'My Nanny O' was at the time uppermost in my mind because at its first appearance the first verse of it was this - 'Behind yon hills where Strichar flows'. Sugar has however been substituted for Strichar, and is more euphonious. Ayrshire has been rendered classic ground by the genius of Burns. Soon after I examined a sort of spade which I found in a lime cart, and which I believe is peculiar to Ayrshire. About a mile from the village I found several specimens of a plant which I found to be the Common Sheep's-bit, a pretty little plant having the habit of a Scabious, and hence named in English Sheep's Scabius. The road leaves the sea not far from Ballintrae, and passes over hills covered with heath for several miles. The interior now bore a different aspect from what it had hitherto done. It consists of heathy hills, some of which were pretty high, being according to my estimation about 1500 feet above the sea. After passing over a piece of heath nearly four miles in extent I came upon a valley which bore a striking resemblance to the glens of the highlands.

About eight and a half miles from Ballintrae, and at the mouth of Glenappe I again came to the sea, which here appeared in the form of a loch, or inlet. It is named Loch Ryan and is about twelve miles in length, and at an average about three in breadth. On the opposite or western side I saw the land low and cultivated, unlike that on the eastern which is hilly and sterile, excepting along the shore, partaking of the nature of the land over which I had just passed. Looking toward the mouth of the Loch I saw the coast of Ireland at a great distance, obscured by mist. The scenery is not interesting because same and uniform; yet not absolutely dull or disagreeable. The road passes along the shore of the lake all the way to Stranraer which is situated at its extremity. The shore in all this course is pebbly excepting in a few places where it is composed of low rocks. There is little wood and the trees appear stunted and unhealthy probably owing to the sea air. About two miles from the mouth of Glenappe, I found the Orpine growing very abundantly on the pebbly beaches. This is the first time I have seen it growing wild though I had examined it before from a garden specimen. The other plants which I observed on the beaches were the Sea Campion, White English Stonecrop, Spreading Halbert-shaped Orache, Common Wild Chamomile, and Silver-weed. On the top, and at the foot of an old wall near the village of Cairn Ryan six miles distant from Stranraer I found the Dwarf Sea Wheat-grass in abundance. This is a rare plant, and I have only seen it elsewhere in the Island of Harris. Near this village I also found the Dwarf Mallow, which I had seen before only in the Botanic Garden at Glasgow. It was here abundant. The other remarkable plants which occurred by the road were the Yellow-iris, Common Thrift, Sea Plantain, Great Water Plantain, Common Gorse, and Wild Carrot. The Gorse was plentiful. In a little marsh about two miles from Stranraer I observed the following plants; Mare's-tail, Marsh Trefoil, Yellow-iris, Sharp-flowered Rush, Floating Bur-reed, Marsh Penny, and Yellow water-lily, constituting a fine little collection of water plants.

The birds seen today were but few, they were of the following species; Magpie, Common Gull, Robin, Pied Wagtail, Heron, Hedge Sparrow, Yellow Hammer, Linnet, Swallow, Chough, Chaffinch, and House Sparrow.

Of the Chough I am not sure. I had seen birds of the species in the Isles of Barray in 1818 but am not familiar enough with it to recognise it by its mode of flying and notes. The cows which I saw in the hill part of Ayrshire differed from those of the low country in being less sleek, and generally of a black colour. Most of them wanted horns. Soon after leaving Glenappe I entered Wigtownshire in which I now am. I arrived at Stranraer in the dusk. Today I have only travelled eighteen miles, but there is a great difference between travelling like a common pedestrian, and like a student of Natural History. I am generally obliged to sit up till after twelve writing my notes, and this prevents me getting off at an early hour. The inhabitants of Ayrshire are in general well-formed. There is an agreeable openness in their countenance, very different from the expression of those of the people about Glasgow. The women are good-looking, some of them I have seen even pretty, but none enchanting. Many of the women wear a large, clumsy tartan plaid about their shoulders, with the ends crossed before and hanging down nearly to the ground. Those about Paisley wore grey cloaks which covered their heads. One feels pleased to find a general peculiarity in dress or manners pervading a district. In civilised countries however national or provincial peculiarities in dress are seldom to be found, excepting among the peasantry. In Lewis and Harris the women wear a short square piece of tartan about their shoulders, fastened before by a circular silver brooch. It is infinitely more becoming than the large plaid of the Ayrshire women, or the plain red or tartan plaid of the old wives of Aberdeenshire covering the head, shoulders, and waist, or the grey cloak of Renfrewshire, or the blue one of Inverness concealing the figure and face. Since the unfortunate battle of Culloden the kilt has become almost extinct in the Highlands. This perhaps is not very much to be regretted. But even tartan has come into disuse. Instead of the plumed bonnet, short coat, feilebeg waistcoat and hose of tartan, the graceful plaid, the dirk, pistols, and claymore of former times, we have now in the highlands the Saxon dress in all its ridiculous varieties. The very breeches which the highlanders once detested of all things, are now common among the peasantry about Inverness. Near the mouth of Glenappe, on the side of Loch Ryan, I found a plant which I carried here with me. It is the Hemp Agrimony.

Stranraer, Thursday evening 29th September 1819

I could scarcely prevail upon myself to get into bed this morning at one o'clock. The consequence was that I slept till ten. Soon after I proceeded to Portpatrick which is distant from this by a short road, about six miles. About a mile and a half from town I washed my face and hands in a rivulet by the road. As I was returning to the highway I was accosted by a man with "Come are ye for this road, lad?" Yes, I replied, but I walk alone. "Eh?" I always walk alone. Y'ere maybe best alone, said he. Yes said I. Oh, I thought ye were for company - like me, said the fellow looking down very complacently on his new corduroy breeches and white worsted stockings. No, replied I firmly. "Ah, weel-weel". He was not a vicious looking fellow by any means, but just such as in Aberdeenshire is called 'an honest-like man', that is a great lump of a flab-fleshed fellow just like a vast haggis or a bag of sheepskin stuffed with porridge. This leads me, by the way, to observe that it is my custom always by night as well as by day to walk alone. I cannot bear to be disturbed in my meditations. And the conversation of the generality of pedestrian travellers is by no means in my estimation sufficient to compensate the loss of the precious produce of the cogitative fermentation of my own ideas. People who cannot think for themselves feel melancholy, or at least uneasy if they cannot find company. As to myself I am never more employed than when i am left alone. Since I left Aberdeen I have not walked four miles altogether in company of any living wight. But I am never actually alone, for whenever I choose I can summon up a band of imaginary beings suited to my temper and disposition for the time. In Kirk Alloway I had the spirits of Burns, Sterne and Goethe, when crossing the Strichar the ideal form of the beautiful, simple, innocent charming nanny accompanied me. At Portpatrick I saw on the beach 'a poor exile of Erin' with the chilling dewdrops upon his threadbare garment. The whistling of the wind among the grass of a highland valley and the grey stones of the desert call to my mind the ancient heroes of Albyn. In the blasted oak of the mountain I see the form of Ossian, the last of a noble race. The roar of the brown torrent in the lone valley, the rustling of the ferns, and the distant roar of the ocean sounding sad in the blast, call to my mind the image of the aged bard, blind, forsaken, and broken-hearted, left in the house of the stranger, the sport of 'the sons of little men' (Ossian). What heart of even common sensibility does not thrill in anguish, and feel the 'melancholy joy of grief' during the perusal of the pathetic tales of this illustrious bard (Ossian) delivered with that noble simplicity which alone accords with nature. Let anyone compare the poems of Ossian or of Burns, or 'The Sorrows of Wester' or Zimmerman's Essay on Solitude or Lavater's Essays, with Miss Porter's Scottish Chiefs, and he will perceive the superiority of simplicity of diction. But I am beginning to wander from my subject. The sight of the mountain brings along with it the hunters of Morven, the fair-haired Oscar of the mighty deeds, with the blue-eyed maids of Selma. There is a voice in the wild and lonely waste that speaks to my soul of vast and boundless eternity. The past and the future are blended, time becomes a mere relative idea, not an actual entity, and my spirit dashes through the immeasurable realms of space and eternity. I feel myself expand, but these ideas cannot be expressed, and were they even delineated to my satisfaction they would not be understood, but would leave the reader to think me a weak visionary enthusiast. So I am perhaps, or worse.

Now how could I think of substituting for such companions as these the conversation of some poor degraded being of my species who enjoys perhaps little more than a mere sensitive existence, and whose questions and remarks occasion in me a continual war between benevolence and peevishness. There are times for all things however as Solomon rather too unconditionally remarks, and from the conversation of the meanest and the actions of the vilest one may learn much. And I have learned much from them, if in truth I may say I have learned much of anything, excepting folly. Sometime before I come to the end of my journey I shall alter my present plan and then we shall have remarks of a different nature. We, I say for my readers accompany me everywhere, that is, such of them as I know, and there are six or seven of them for whom I have respect or esteem, or love, or some sensation composed of these and of a desire to please and to be of service by pointing out in my own conduct the errors into which a person of tolerable literary education, some sensibility, some acuteness, but withal devoid of firmness, is likely to fall.

I arrived about one o'clock at Portpatrick where the ferry to Ireland is. My intention was to step into one of the packet boats, and after writing a chapter beginning with 'The waters heave around me, and the winds lift up their voices' (Childe Harold) to land at Donaghadee, sleep a night in Ireland, and return next day to proceed on my journey. The sea was very high, and the winds boisterous and contrary, and although three of the boats were lying in the harbour, none of them could venture out. I went into an Inn and drank a little whisky, and dined with a whole crew of sailors. The landlady sat at table to deal out his allowance to each. I have not seen a more interesting woman since I left Aberdeen. She was young, handsome, neat, modest, pretty, very polite, and extremely kind and obliging, and had a slight tinge of the Irish brogue which appeared in her very agreeable, though I never deemed it to be so in any other person. After dining I felt melancholy, not melancholy but impatient, and determined not to remain there all night to wait a chance of getting to Ireland next day, but to return I walked a while upon the shore. The rocks and pasture grounds were like those of the Island of Harris, and I became melancholy, and I returned instantly to the Inn, and threw my napsack on my shoulders, and paid the landlady, and sallied forth. The wind was fair with me, and I got here in the dusk. Portpatrick is a small town, or rather a pretty large village. The houses are in general neat and slated. Almost every house is an Inn or a receptacle of provisions, or 'British spirits, porter, and ale'. It was crowded with poor Irishmen waiting for a passage. Great swarms of Hibernians emigrate into the southwest of Scotland, and one fourth of the inhabitants of Glasgow it is said are Irishmen. They are not liked by the Scotch, but I am inclined to think they are treated unfairly, and that the generality of them are by no means bad fellows. I am of opinion that an essay on signs and sign boards would afford amusement. Perhaps it may sooner or later be forthcoming. Tonight I observed on a board in this town DRY LODGINGS by ELS MATTHEWS. The country between this and Portpatrick is in many places heathy resembling Bracadale in Skye. The harbour is very small and is formed principally by a pier built between it and the sea. About three eighths of a mile on this side of it I saw in a den the Hemp Agrimony, and at the town the Common Mallow. I have not seen any other rare plants today, excepting the Water Hemlock. Today I saw what I thought an oddish sort of phenomenon. Two jackdaws sitting on the head of a cow, a living cow I mean. The starling was the only bird which I knew that makes a practice of sitting upon cattle. This mention of the starling leads me to think of Sterne's Sentimental Journey, and to reflections on Liberty. There is nothing almost so horrible to me as the idea of being confined in a small cell such as Baron Trencks, of six or seven or eight feet square. And I am convinced that if I were actually cooped up in such I would either dash out my brains against the wall, or work up my sensations and ideas into madness, or break my heart with grief and impatience. Some men bear confinement as well as pigs or geese, and like them fatten in it. When I am put to sleep in a small apartment, if after the light is put out extravagant ideas of liberty come into my mind I am sometimes obliged to leap out of bed. The night I slept at Glasgow I left the gas light burning all night, and I am not afraid that my reader will construe this into superstitious fear, after he has seen me sleeping with the greatest composure in a mountain glen in one of the wildest places of Scotland upwards of eight miles from the nearest house; or lingering in the most horrid glen in Britain till night should fall and 'improve' the scenery 'the wrong way'. Bye the bye I once was terrified at the idea of ghosts and goblins, and would not for a world walk out at night. But the exercise of reflection has completely rooted out every apprehension of that sort. Yet I am, by no means constitutionally brave, and sometimes at night when travelling or sitting out, a sudden sound or appearance near me makes the hair of my head stand erect and my eyes to stare. But this is merely a momentary sensation. I am about to arrogate to myself great merit in regard to this particular. He who is constitutionally brave has no more merit on that account than Aesop had demerit for having a hump. But he who overcomes a natural failing and completely represses the consequence of an extreme sensibility to danger deserves praise, and enjoys a degree of satisfaction of which no dispraise or contempt can ever deprive him. And the mention of satisfaction brings to my remembrance an assertion of Bacon's placed as a motto on the title page of a short account of the Botanic Garden of Glasgow which is this, 'A Garden is the purest of all human pleasures'. Now I maintain that this is a very ridiculous assertion and very unworthy of its author. The purest and highest of all pleasures, at least the purest and the highest of which I am capable, consists of the consciousness of rectitude and the conviction of having done one's duty. And I know and have experienced a pleasure purer and more exquisite than that which a flower garden yields, and I think I am capable of deriving pleasure from a garden as any man in existence, and this pleasure arises from the pure contemplation of female beauty combined with perfect innocence, while at the same time one is confident that he is high in the esteem of this object of his unbounded admiration. I am not sure that the manner in which I have expressed this will enable one to understand it. Be it known that love, at least the affection or combination of affections known by the name of love, is entirely out of the question. Love is a word which has twenty meanings, I cannot rightly define at present the love to which I allude, but I refer three of my readers to a letter written by me to Miss J G to be seen in my account of the summer of 1818. There is another subject on which I must say a few words, it is patience. Patience, praise it who will, I esteem a very bad quality. It is indicative of a disposition inclined to contentment, and of contentment, praise it who will, I wish none. The man of patience is commonly a dull animal whose blood stagnates in his veins like the water in a Dutch canal; and the man of contentment is commonly a foolish, silly, constitutionally good-natured sort of a useless, good-for-nothing creature. Patience may contribute toward serenity, and contentment may yield pleasure. But this serenity and this pleasure are not much elevated above mere animal sanity which is the consequence of the due performance of every primary and subordinate function belonging to the machine. If patience and contentment had been universally diffused we should never have had a Byron, a Sterne, a Linnaeus, a Humboldt - or a single man of genius, and I should never have been the town of Stranraer, the largest in Wigton-shire, so named after a horde of barbers.

Newtown Stewart, Wigton-shire.   Friday evening, 1st October

It rained very heavily this morning and the weather did not clear up till after ten. About eleven I left Stranraer. It is a pretty large, and tolerably well-built town, situated at the head of Loch Ryan. Looking down the loch I saw the Isle of Arran once more opposite its mouth. In a ditch near the town, by the road, I observed the Three-cleft Bur-marigold along with the Biting Persicaria. Nothing very interesting occurred today and I believe I may with great propriety shorten my story and say that I arrived here about seven o'clock. The distance is twenty six miles. In this course only one town occurred, Glenluce, sixteen miles from this. The country is in general heathy, especially on this side of Glenluce. The surface is gently undulated. The elevations are commonly cultivated excepting a few which are pretty high, the ground between them being in most places composed of very deep peat. There are no hawthorn hedges, the fences being all of stone. Few trees also occur. Here I became for the first time sensible of the approach of winter. The brakes were withered, the leaves of the trees are beginning to change their hues, and the grass upon the heath has assumed a yellowish tinge. When I was in Argyllshire nothing of this was perceptible, and everything excepting the stubble fields was green. Few plants are now in flower, and none in perfection. The Common Grass of Parnassus occurred today. I tasted some berries of Bitter-sweet which I found by a dyke. They were gelatinous and had a disagreeable taste and smell, but neither sweetness or bitterness as the name implies. There is an astonishing number of Macs in this country. Today I noticed the following on signboards - MacGaa, MacGeoch, MacElement, MacRory, Macbedie, MacClegg, MacLaren, MacMicken, MacGuyer, MacQuaid. These I believe are all Irish names, as I have never heard or seen any of them in the Highlands. Whins occurred frequently today, but I did not see any broom.

Gatehouse, Kirkcudbright-shire, Saturday 2nd October 11 pm

The feeling of insecurity which a man of an impatient temper has when among vicious people is distressing, more especially at night when the lights are out. In the house in which I lodged last night I found a diabolical countenance. It was expressive of malevolence, irrascibility, and brutal degradation. The forehead was if not the most expressive feature at least the most palpably marked. The eyebrows projected, and the furrows above the root of the nose were deeper than I had ever before seen. It was the face of a female advanced in years. The tempers of the several members of the family appeared to have been moulded to that of this incarnate fiend. Even the very dog of the house was more surly and snappish than the generality of the canine species. In my bedroom there were two beds. One was occupied by a young man of the family and a large dog. I sat up till my candle burnt done. Today I rose about half past eight and soon after breakfasted. At nine I left Newton Stewart. I felt stiffish and was proceeding at a slow pace when I was overtaken by a swaggering fellow who asked "are ye gaun far this way?" Yes, said I, unwilling to let him know how far or where I was going. "How far are ye gaun?" East a good way, answered I. "Eh?" East apiece. He walked onward a few paces, hesitatingly, then half turned about, and muttered the following reason for his questions; "because if you were for company I'm gaun that way too". I walk alone always observed I repressingly as I had done to the man of Port Patrick. Eh? No. About a mile from the town I passed a house above the door of which I observed this inscription 'God's Providence is my inheritance. William Muir 1770'. The reflections which this excited must be referred to another opportunity. Three miles from Newton Stewart I found the Trailing Tormentil by a hedge. I had not seen it before and in Scotland it appears to be a very rare plant.

Sunday morning (in continuation)

The scenery was completely altered. On the left hand were hills covered with fine wood, on the left a fertile plain. Soon after I reached the head of a bay or frith, and along its banks I proceeded until I had got halfway. The road then turned from the main frith along a smaller one, at the head of which is the small town of Gatehouse in which I now am. About 6 miles from Newton Stewart there is a large village upon the frith and by the River Cree which there enters it. It is named Ferrytown or Creetown and on the opposite side I saw the town of Wigton. Between Creetown and this the scenery is interesting, there is a fine view of the bay and coast, and along the hills in the whole course there is a great deal of natural wood, principally oak. Five miles from this place I went off the road to look at some birds upon a pool. In a field over which I passed I found the Wild Carrot abundant and pulled and eat some of its roots. Here also I found in abundance the Common Scarlet Pimpernel and Corn Woundwort. On arriving here I dined in an Inn and then went in search of Mr Miller, Officer of Excise whom I found and with whom I staid last night. His wife is from Aberdeen and I had been aquainted with them when there. Today I rose at seven, and washed from head to foot in a stream near the town. I do not feel disposed somehow for regular narrative, and as I have some remarks to make of importance I shall write a page or two without order. In the first place I shall dispatch my plants of yesterday. The characters of the two species of Tormentilla are not correctly marked by Linnaeus or any other botanists. They are in my opinion the following: T. officianalis T. caulibus decumbente ibus ramosa, foliis sessilibus. T reptans T. caulibus radii antribus simplicibus, foliis petiolatis. In officianalis the leaves are only sub-sessile, and in reptans they are longly petiolated but for the sake of elegance and brevity these minute circumstances cannot find a place in the specific character.

The fruit of the Blackthorn is of a bluish-purple colour, often obscured by a white mealy substance. Its taste is acid and astringent. The fruit of the Common Bramble is black tinged with blue. It is not very agreeable to the taste but has a slight degree of astringency. It is more sweet than acid, but a narcotic taste is also perceptible. When eaten in considerable quantity bramble berries produce nausea. The fruit of the Hawthorn is red and with a sub-astringent and rather disagreeable taste. These together with the hazlenut, raspberry and strawberry are the chief fruits of the south of Scotland. The Common Grass of Parnassus, Great Bindweed, Hemp Agrimony, Yellow-iris, Perennial Mercury, Tutsan, and the Great Water Plaintain, occurred yesterday. The Common Reed is common here in ditches by the road. The beautiful Spiked Purple Loose-strife is also common, as well as the Common Sheep's-bit. The Yellow-iris is very common in the Western Isles, and from Fort William to this place I have found it here and there. The plants which I have added to my lift from yesterday's observations are the Corn Woundwort and Hard Rush.

In the house in which I lodged at Newton Stewart I was no sooner seated than my attention was attracted by a chirping behind the fireplace. I asked of the devil-faced hag if they had got young birds there. She answered that it was the crickets. It was the first time I had heard this little animal. It was the first time too that I thought it improper to laugh at Dr. Johnston for his wonder on seeing some cockles and limpets in the Isle of Skye. The more that a person knows the less apt will he be to ridicule the ignorance of others. Everyone qualified to use his eyes aright may have observed that those who are themselves very ignorant are always very ready to apply ridicule to the blunders of others more ignorant. Ridicule when used without the motive of a desire to reform is indicative of a vicious, and in certain circumstances, of a diabolic disposition. Ridicule or derision pointed against a person not vicious but awkward or diffident and bashful, and pointed too so as to be discovered by the poor booby himself is of this kind. This sort of ridicule I have experienced, but only once in my life, and I considered the person a despicable creature. I have certainly very often been in circumstances which could not fail to excite ridicule in others, but either good manners, as they are called, or benevolence restrained every palpable indication of it. My blunders have not arisen so much from ignorance but from extreme diffidence, an almost insuperable fear of not being able to acquit myself properly. Henceforth therefore I shall not laugh at Dr Johnson's account of limpets, although I may at my own at mistaking the chirping of crickets for that of a bird. Mr Miller accompanied me last night to an oven in this town where I obtained two of them which I have put into two small boxes. They are quite harmless and their cry is not disagreeable. It is pleasing to reflect that one is always adding to his knowledge - but three days ago I did not know that there were crickets in Scotland. I have not yet learned how to give a proper answer to a vulgar ignorant person who asks what use I make of my plants. Perhaps in such a case I might even be justified in saying "my good friend, that is a subject which cannot be in any respect interesting to you". Yesterday as I was trudging along with a bundle of plants in my hand, a woman took the liberty of asking "Is that yerbs?" Yes answered I. Ow! that's rushes, exclaimed she with a stupid sort of surprise. Yes, said I, it is a kind of rush (It was Hard Rush). Fat's this, continued my queries taking hold of another plant, I don't know the English name of it replied I rather foolishly; are ye gaun ti' drink affin't? no I don't intend to put it to any medical use. The Birds which occurred yesterday were the following species: Magpie, House Sparrow, Hedge Sparrow, Cross-bill, Yellow Hammer, Skylark, Meadow Pipit, Jackdaw, Rook, Crow, Woodpigeon, Robin, Whinchat, Wren, Comon Gull, and Curlew.

Kirkcudbrightshire   Monday 4th October 11 pm

I am now in the house of a farmer about four miles to the eastward of Castle Douglas on the Dumfries road. I have been conducted by the good woman to my bedroom, at a table in which I am seated. It is a tolerable apartment about 20 feet square and 8 in height. In one corner is a bed with old-fashioned red homespun curtains. This bed is furnished with a chaff and feather bed, three pairs of Scotch blankets, a clean white cover, and a pillow and bolster, all neatly arranged and fitted by the hands of the landlady for the reception of the unworthy carcasse of the descendant of the 'man of the hillside'. Between the bed and the door is a large red press the contents of which it does not become me to scrutinise. On the floor is a very old and very bare carpet, and around the room are arranged half a dozen of common and two arm chairs of beech wood, I believe with fir bottoms. The table is also of beech. On one side is a chest of drawers on the top of which are deposited Brown's dictionary of the Bible, and five numbers of some religious work the titles of which are 'A soul prepared for heaven, the watchful Christian dying in peace, surprise in death, the wrath of the lamb, the vain refuge of sinners, and no night in heaven'. Along with these is a tea-canister and above them on the wall hangs a black velvet woman's bonnet. The fireplace which has a good cast metal grate is flanked on each side with a press painted red. In one of them I suspect is contained a shake-down bed. On the chimney piece are placed two volumes of an edition of Burn's works, a pocket bible in two volumes, memoirs of the Princess Charlotte, and The Saint's Everlasting Rest, written by the reverend pious and learned Mr Richard Baxter. In the rear of these and in contact with the wall is a great radiated bundle of peacock's feathers. Above this arranged nearly in a straight line are placed sixteen pockets of a triangular shape made, some of satin, some of paper, some of straw, and all very tastefully decorated with knots of ribbons of a hundred various hues. These sixteen pockets, pouches, or purses are the receptacles of the stalkends of sixteen bundles of corn, principally oats. Each of them has a name and date upon it, for example, Janet Dempster, Sept 25, 1815, Mr Robert Shaw Isles, Sept 2, 1815, John Carson, Sept 25, 1812. The walls are painted one half with yellow ochre, the other with whitening tinged with indigo. There are two windows, both curtained with muslin, and in one of them is a tea tray. But to tell my story rightly I must return to Gatehouse. I arrived there as has been said on Saturday evening. Mr Miller entertained me with the sort of hospitality which I had often experienced in the Isles of the West, and in his house I remained till today about one o'clock. Yesterday I wrote a little and examined some plants, and today I pasted thirty-two specimens of plants upon large paper. Mr Miller accompanied me, upon duty, about four miles. The weather was very fine, about half past five I reached the small town of Castle-Douglas, fifteen miles from Gatehouse. It was my intention to have remained there but the beds of the inns were all occupied on account of there having been a market in the neighbourhood, and I proceeded. In the dusk I overtook a man on horseback, who soon after directed me to take a shortcut to avoid a doubling of the road. I hesitated at first, but judging the man by his voice and manner to be an honest fellow I followed his directions. Soon after he overtook me, and we had a desultory sort of conversation which produced an invitation to accept a bed and pot luck in a farmer's house - a plain farmer he added, and no lard or landholder. This invitation I accepted with great glee for the nearest inn I was informed was six miles off, and after all a bad one. So about half a mile off the road we came to the house. After warming ourselves at a large peat fire placed on the floor as the fires generally are in the Isles, we ate a hearty meal, and soon after retired severally to our bedrooms. In the kitchen where I had warmed myself I saw a woman quite in the style of Meg Merilees. She had been a soldier's wife and had lost her husband and five sons in the wars. Her diction was fluent, and not coarse or inelegant, and she gesticulated with great propriety and energy. She had been lately in England, and her account of the riots in Manchester was most amusing. Her remarks upon tythes and the 'black-bottomed bishops' of England were also amusing, and she narrated her own misfortunes quite in the oriental style of story-telling. The landlord informed me as a little cracked in the noddle. I have not seen a person who interests me more since I left Aberdeen. She would make a noble subject for the pencil or the pen. The country over which I have passed today is well-cultivated and fertile. The surface is very unequal but in no place do the hills rise to any considerable height. The sea was not in view. In general therefore the country is not picturesque, the view being too limited, and there being too much sameness in the scenery. In one place however I had a fine scene. It was on the banks of the large river which falls into the sea at Kirkudbright. For several miles along its banks a fine open plain was seen extending northward and in the distance mountains tipped with clouds. At Castle-Douglas there is a lake nearly a mile in length, but its banks are not interesting. I saw a cormorant today flying near a river by the road, and a magpie sitting on a cow. No rare plants occurred. Whins are common, hawthorn is used for fences, and though there are no extensive woods the country does not by any means look bare, as there are single trees and sometimes clumps scattered here and there.

Dumfries. Tuesday 5th October 3 PM

In the morning I was awakened by my host who came to desire me to rise and get some breakfast. My papers were lying on the table, and after applying his spectacles to his nose he looked at some of them. In due time I was conducted to the parlour, which was also used as a bedroom, where I found the landlady and her daughter and a mason or mechanic of some sort or other. The good people had no notions of gentility, as it is called. The girl was young and handsome and had the physiognomic marks of good nature and modesty, and appeared capable of being transformed into a very interesting young woman. But like the rest, she was a complete rustic. To a highlander who has never travelled, the difference of manners between his country-men and the lowlanders appears very striking. In the Highlands, universally about fifty years ago, and even at the present day in several extensive districts, there were only three classes of people - the chieftains or lairds, the tacksmen, and the tenantry. The tacksmen were commonly, but not always related in some degree to the chief and rented from him a large portion of land. This they occupied in part, and sublet in part to the tenants. Each tacksman was a sort of chieftain upon his own farm, and was much more respected than a lowlander can easily conceive. The same homage was paid by him to his chief. In regard to education, no difference existed between the families of the chiefs and those of the tacksmen. The males of both got a genteel and learned education, and most of them went through the usual course of some one of the

Universities of Edinburgh, Glasgow, or Aberdeen, particularly those of Edinburgh or King's College at Aberdeen. The females in some instances were educated in Edinburgh or Glasgow - and those who were brought up at home were taught to hold vulgarity of every kind in the utmost abhorrence. Between the family of the tacksman who paid a rent of three hundred pounds and of him who paid only sixty there was no difference. They were all equally genteel, equally respected by their inferiors, and equally esteemed by each other. In this condition, Dr Johnson found the tacksmen of Skye, and his remarks, in spite of the prejudice and ignorance with which they are structured, are calculated to impress a high idea of them. In this condition they still remain in the Islands of Skye, Lewes, Harris, Uist, and Barray. The man, who if placed in the low country, would be esteemed a poor farmer is absolutely a gentleman, and proprietors of extensive districts in the lowlands may be found who are far inferior to an islander who rents a small farm of a hundred pounds a year. The opulence of the farmer in whose home I was last night, would in the Isles produce a degree of gentility scarcely credible. The social virtues of the Highlander too are infinitely superior to those of the Lowlanders. Wherever their name is known they are famed for their hospitality, and their incorruptible fidelity to their friends. The impetuous exertion of affection which I have seen manifested among friends in the Highlands would make the Lowlanders of most districts stare with astonishment. I think I am not prejudiced; for I am neither a Lowlander nor a Highlander - but a something between the two. Yet I may truly say in the words of the old song 'My heart's in the Highlands wherever I go'. After breakfast I continued my journey and arrived here about half past three, the distance being fifteen miles. The country is well cultivated and the same nature as that over which I passed yesterday, but less agreeable as the hedges are substituted by stone fences, and there is scarcely any wood. No rare plants occurred. Very few are now in flower and Flora has withdrawn her smiles from Albyn to bestow then on more southern climes. The birds which occurred today were of the following species; Coal Tit, Reed Bunting, Chaffinch, Magpie, Skylark, Meadow Pipit, Rook, Pied Wagtail, Robin, House Sparrow, Yellow Hammer, Whinchat, and Swallow.

The Meadow Pipit is more generally spread over Scotland than any other bird. It occurs in every sort of situation; in cornfields, pastures and woods, by the sea shore and on the heaths, even in the central part as well in the isles as on the mainland. The Robin is also very generally diffused over the mainland, but as it lives principally among bushes and thickets it not be seen in any part of the Long Island. About a mile from Dumfries I saw a weasel. The quadrupeds of Scotland are very few in number. In as far as I know, the following list comprehends them all; Common Seal, Grey Seal, Wild Cat, Red Deer, Brown Rat, Roe Deer, Fox, Black Rat, Mountain Hare, Brown Hare, Otter, House Mouse, Field Mouse, Stoat, Weasel, Shrew, Polecat, Badger, Pine Marten, Water Shrew.

8 o'clock. In the dusk I went out with the intention of visiting the grave of Burns. I sauntered about the town for some time looking for a churchyard but I saw none. I hesitated whether I should search longer for it or not. I felt somewhat melancholy, and had almost determined to return to the Inn, but a thought struck me. The grave of Burns, thought I, could I possibly pass it over. Ideas were associated with grave which I cannot define, nor where they indeed definite, they were but the faint shadows of ideas. At length I found the old churchyard near the town in which I was informed the monument was. The gate was shut, but I cannot bear the idea of little artificial restraints of this kind and having found a place where the wall was not very high, I clambered over it, and was presently among a wilderness of tombs. I had never before see a spot of earth as thickly tenanted. I proceeded in search of the monument, but hundreds appeared on all sides. At length I spied one more magnificent than the rest and approached it. It was in the form of a dome supported by eight Ionic pillars. Through the iron railings I could distinguish the figure of a man holding a plough in white marble. This is it said I, and before I had reached the outer gate I burst into tears. The monument was enclosed by a stone wall, on the top of which was an iron railing, and the gate was locked. While looking round to see if I could find an opening, I observed a board which intimated that the Magistrate had determined to lodge in jail any person convicted of leaping over the walls. I found no opening. What thought I, have I to do with restraint. These walls were not intended to exclude me, for the memory of the poet is dear to my heart, and I could not injure his monument. So I got over the railing and sat down on the steps. I again burst into tears. My ideas were not precisely defined, and passion does not vent itself in 'set speeches'. The only words which broke forth at intervals between my sobs were - poor unfortunate Burns. My ideas were wild and melancholy and I felt bewildered, in a labyrinth which I have never been able to trace. It was nearly dark by this time. Would to heaven, said I, that some spirit would appear before me and remove my doubts. But these phantoms of the weak and superstitious mind are not to be seen by me. Is it possible, thought I, that the spirit of Burns could be doomed to eternal misery, while that of some dull hypochondriac is - the idea appeared inadmissible. Yet if there be no difference between the soul of a Burns and of an idiot, I would not comprehend it. A confusion of ideas succeeded, and the wild vortex of undefined and unutterable thoughts which I have so often experienced, jumbled all perceptions and sensations. In this frenzy I dared to address the Supreme Being. Merciful God! said I, kneeling on the steps of the monument, grant me a ray of heavenly light to guide my steps through this vale of misery. It is, I believe, half a year since I addressed the deity before, and I am not by any means convinced of the propriety of doing it at this time. However I felt calmer, and seating me again upon the steps fell into a state of soft melancholy. The idea of Burns again occupied my mind. I felt that his very memory was dearer to me than any living being (of my own sex). I know not what attaches me so closely to this child of nature, but I think that a great deal of my attachment depends upon his misfortunes and his untimely fate. There is a stage in the paroxysm of grief which to me is highly pleasing. The acme was past. I reflected on my situation. The shades of darkness were blended with those of twilight, I was alone in the mansion of the dead. The bodies of my fellow men were mouldering around me, I was removed from the world, from its vices and vanities. I was inspired by the pure spirit of melancholy, I felt the joy of grief, and I exclaimed "I would not exchange the pure bliss of this hour, for all the joys which Fortune bestows on her favourites". I dried up my tears with my handkerchief and proceeded to the place where I had ascended the wall, but I found the stones at the top very loose, and did not venture. At length I found a low part of the wall and dropped into the street.

Perhaps my readers may imagine, that having been a medical student, I am well versed in the art of climbing the walls of churchyards. But, in justice to the memory of William MacGillivray late student of medicine at Aberdeen, I must assure them that he never once entered a burial place with the intention of feloniously removing from thence the deserted carcasse of any human being. No, by heaven, I have too much regard for the sacred feelings of the children of affliction, and too great an abhorrence of the mean crime of stealing, to be able to pilfer a dead body. Yet I know a young man who even stole a body with the sole intention of selling it, and sell it he did, and obtained six guineas for it. And the young man is in a lucrative situation, and is perhaps respected by his neighbours, while I, poor, neglected and forlorn, am wandering over the world - 'the exile of my own dark mind' (Byron) an object of compassion to my friends, of ridicule, to my enemies, if I have any, for I take God to witness that I have no serious enmity against any of my fellow creatures.

11 o'clock. 'Past eleven o'clock - a cloudy night' cries a watchman on the street. I have just finished some drawings, and now proceed to dispatch a few unconnected remarks and observations.

Clogs - Dumfries clogs. I saw the sign in shop windows in several towns by the way. What can this mean? said I. At length I learned that clogs are a sort of shoe with a very thick wooden sole. In this country they are worn by men and women alike, but only by the poorer sort. The soles are generally upwards of an inch in thickness and are covered with iron plates. They raise a disagreeable clatter on the streets and from their not bending render a person's motions awkward. I am told they are much more comfortable than shoes - and this I readily believe, because they elevate the foot above the mud. I wonder if they be the same as the sabots of the French peasantry. In this country a three-forked spade, like Neptune's trident is used for lifting potatoes. In some of the Western Isles a small instrument with two incurvated prongs capable of being wielded by one hand is used. This suggested to me the figure of an instrument I got made for lifting the roots of plants, and which is in every respect superior to a small spade or trowel of any description. The long-stalked spade which I thought peculiar to Ayrshire is common in Wigton and Kirkcudbrightshires. It is by no means equal to the common spade because it requires more power, and after all has not nearly the same effect. Figures of these will be annexed.

I mentioned as a conjecture sometime near the beginning of my journey that in the west of Scotland, meaning that part of the West Highlands which I intended to visit, I should be taken for a pedlar. There, however, I was generally thought a land surveyor, or a person looking after curiosities, and sent out for that purpose by some society, for they could not comprehend how I should travel so much merely from inclination. Between Glasgow and this place I have always at first been considered as a pedlar, or a book-man. When I informed my host of last night that I looked principally after plants, he laughed heartily and observed that it was a simple thing, meaning that botany in his conception is an insignificant study. This leads me to remark that the ideas of mankind are not similar on any one subject whatever. My hostess of last night told me that my handwriting is almost illegible and too small, and in several places I have been asked if it was shorthand which I wrote, because it appeared so small and cramped. Now most people of education consider my writing as very plain, and upon the whole very good, and this truly is my own opinion of it, though I am not by any means satisfied with it and intend to improve it greatly. Nor is there any subject whatever regarding which the opinions of all men coincide. What one nation considers a virtue, the other considers a vice. Every point in religion is the same. Amid so great a diversity of opinion is it possible that one form of religion should be instituted by divine authority - that its observance should be strictly enjoined and absolutely necessary for salvation, and yet that it should be confined to less than the hundredth part of the inhabitants of the earth. On the other hand was it not probably, necessary amid so great a diversity of opinion to institute a fine form of religion to which all nations should in time conform. Is this form of religion preserved prime by those who have adopted it? Is there not on the contrary as great a difference between the doctrines of the two most opposite sects as between the religion of Brama and that of Mahomet? Is the virtue of mankind greatly improved by this religion? Are the Catholics of France or the Protestants of Germany superior in virtues to the Ancient Greeks and Romans when in their noblest condition? And if those who profess it, do not render their conduct conformable to its precepts, what is its use? Philosophers make a great fuss about the monstrous absurdity of scepticism and a still greater one about the inconceivability of atheism, and as Christians, they are perhaps in the right to do so. But as philosophers they ought to consider the subject calmly, and to substitute argument for invective. If a system lead or appear to lead to atheism, it is pronounced absurd, and to show that it leads to this is in philosophy, the equivalent to the reductio ad absurdum of logic. I have seen people who would not think of religion, but were determined to adhere to that which they had, be it right or wrong. And happy it is for those who after being long tossed on the stormy ocean of doubt, at length gain a safe haven. As to me I can only at times exclaim

> Majestic Nature, thous hast charms to smooth
> The mountain billows of that ocean vast
> Where Hope's bewildered barque is darkling tossed.

It is hope which reconciles us to life amid the greatest misfortunes. Without hope, and without woman, man would be a devil, without either of them he might be virtuous, but he would be miserable.

Annan, Dumfries-shire, Wednesday, 6th October, 9 pm.

Yesterday the weather was very fine. There was an exhilarating keen-ness in the air and I trudged along cheerily. Today it rained until about twelve o'clock so that it was near one when I left the Swan Inn at Dumfries, where I had been very well treated. I proceeded along the principal street till I had passed the Old Church. On enquiring here for the Annan road I was informed that I had gone far out of the way, so I returned to the centre of the town, where I received directions. It was at this time about one o'clock. On the wall of the churchyard near which I found myself in a wrong course I found an inscription which I copied. At the head it had the figure of a skull with a semicircular memento mori. On one side two thigh bones crossed and on the other was an hour glass.

PARIES AD
VIATOREM
FABELLA BULLA VITA NIMBUS VANITANS
FLOS FUMUS UMBRA SOMNIUM
HINC ERGO FLUXA AETATIS ECCE CLEPSYDRA
IN OSSA SOLVOR ARIDA
INCERTA CERTA MORTIS HORA TE PRE
S* VIVE DISCAS UT MORI *

* MacGillivray does not explain why the last line is not complete. The missing letters may have been indecipherable.

For nearly six miles from Dumfries the road passes across a large cultivated plain on which the town stands, bounded on the west, north and east by a range of hills, to appearance semi-circular. Though the Solway Frith is not far distant it is not seen on account of some rising ground. Near the centre of this plain is a long piece of heath which extends to the sea, a river of no great size runs along it. After coming to the sixth milestone I found the country composed of low, cultivated hills. Here I had a view of the Solway Frith, and of Cumberland on the English side. Two mountains of considerable elevation appeared among others of less height, but they were enveloped in mist and tipped with clouds, so that their outlines were not defined. The country continued of the same character until I reached Annan. The distance between the two towns is fifteen miles. In all this course the country is well cultivated, and the scenery tolerable, The fences are universally of hawthorn, and there is a good deal of wood, although in no place did I see extensive tracts of it. Near the town I saw two partridges and three pheasants. One of the latter ran across the road before me. I had never before seen a pheasant alive. Few birds occurred today, the weather being gloomy. I had intended to mark all the plants observed today but I found that at the rate of travelling so as to observe plants it would be very late before I would get to Annan, and when I had got four miles from Dumfries I desisted. The leaves are now beginning to fall from the trees, at least from the Hawthorn. No plants appear to be in full flower excepting the Autumnal Hawkbit and perhaps the Common Chickweed.

I had been thinking to begin this day's account in the style of the short chapter written opposite Ailsa in Ayr-shire, and to say - The clatter of clogs is around me - large men's clogs cost five shillings, women's three shillings. They last commonly about two years, but the iron on the soles must be renewed. This iron consists of two pieces for each clog, both marginal, the one on the heel, the other on the toe and halfway to the heel. These pieces of iron are called caulkers. They cost, for both clogs, sixpence. Clogs are not made by the shoemakers, but have given rise to a distinct trade. They are made larger than the foot, and the vacancy is filled with straw. As they do not bend in the sole, the heel rises and falls in them, and thus they wear twice the number of stockings that shoes do. They are very comfortable according to accounts, and I propose, if I return to Aberdeen, to have a pair of them for shooting excursions on the links and other wet places.

A figure is annexed.

Tomorrow I shall enter England.

Spring-field, Thursday 7th October, Noon

I had wished to write my last report while in Scotland of Gretna, or Graitney, celebrated as Denholm remarks in his 'Tour to the lakes' in the annals of clandestine marriage. When I reached this village I thought I had come to Graitney and entered an Inn, but on enquiry I found that Graitney is a quarter of a mile off. It is a matter of little consequence however. I have just finished my breakfast which consisted of two pence worth of bread and a gill of whisky. The reason of my not taking a regular meal was that I had come to the end of one half of the money which I had when leaving Aberdeen, and I wished to begin a new account on entering England. I have now travelled about 500 miles and have been thirty days on my journey. My expenses have been moderate, for I have seldom eaten oftener than twice a day, and I have just expended five pounds sterling. I have only an equal sum remaining, and with this I propose to go to London, to stay there upwards of a week and return to Aberdeen. I would readily undertake a wager to travel to London upon twenty shillings, but I shall not determine the sum, only I shall use the strictest economy. Bread and water will do very well for the greater part of my journey, for many a better man has lived a longer period than will be allotted to it, on worse fare. I have already travelled upwards of five hundred miles, as I have said;

From Aberdeen to Fortwilliam	161 miles
From Fortwilliam to Glasgow	134
From Glasgow to Portpatrick	99
From Portpatrick	109
From Aberdeen to this place	503 miles

It has rained incessantly today, and I am wetted to the skin. I must continue to travel however until I get upon English ground, that I may not be obliged to break upon the remaining half of my money. I am not in a proper mood for making reflections, as may readily be conceived after what I have said. I leave Scotland without regret - Scotland is too wide a word for me as the saying is. It is to the Isles of the west alone that I feel attached, and to the mountains of Albyn, and I pass from Dumfries-shire to Cumberland with perfect unconcern. Excepting the scenes of my youth, the world is all alike to me, its inhabitants are all alike my brethren.

> 'Land of brown heath and shaggy wood,
> Land of the mountain and the flood,
> Land of my sires'

Wherever I go my heart shall still be attached to thee, I dare not awake the remembrance of the days that have been, else we should have a scene like that at the grave of Burns. Then Scotia farewell, 'and if for ever' ---------

Cumberland Friday 8th October 1819   p145

The first object which attracted my attention on entering England was a pig. Some of my own countrymen however resemble this animal just as much as the English. I remember when in the streets of Dundee last spring I saw a baillie looking citizen puffing and sweating under the load of a huge belly. I muttered to myself; I would not carry such a bag as that for a thousand pounds a year. The English however are esteemed men of the highest order. I have not yet learned in what respect an Englishman excels a Scotchman. Is it in personal prowess, in agility, in bravery, in fortitude? Is it in mental acumen, in sociality, in attachment to his country and friends, in sensibility, in honesty, in honour, in virtue, in strict regard to religion, or of what does the superiority of the Englishman consist? I may grow wiser as I proceed. After passing over two or three miles of the debatable ground I crossed the River Esk by a bridge of five arches, and entered Longtown, a large village on its banks. I then proceeded my way to Carlisle where I arrived about five o'clock. The country was flat, and cultivated and divided into small enclosures. Carlisle is a pretty large town, and was formerly walled. There is a castle in its vicinity, a very ugly mass built of red sandstone. It has a cathedral too of the same stone situated on an emminence within the town. The houses are pretty good, but don't look well being built either of red sandstone or brick. Some of them were painted, and in such a case as this painting is allowable. The houses of the peasantry between Longtown and Carlisle are built of straw and mortar. and in general white-washed or painted on the outside. At Carlisle I got at the Bank five English notes in exchange. As I was determined to be economical I did not go to a large Inn, but searched among the smaller sort for lodging but could find none, nor could I get change for one of my notes. I proceeded and marched along the Keswick road till about seven o'clock. I then entered a publick house, but was refused lodging. About half a mile further on I entered another. They had no beds. I ordered supper however, for by this time I was hungry having eaten nothing all day, but a two penny cake. Previously to the good woman's beginning to prepare it I informed her that unless she could give me change she needed not bear the trouble as I had no silver. She said she could give me change, but on my mentioning that my note was of the Bank of England a new difficulty arose, for none of them she said were taken in Cumberland on account of forgeries which had been made. It was in vain that I told them I had got my notes at the Bank. Her husband said that I indeed spoke like an honest man, but that had once been cheated and had resolved never to take again a Bank of England note. I told them I should not have cared upon another occasion, but then I was hungry and fatigued, and could scarcely proceed on my journey. No matter, it wouldn't do - and on I trudged. The road in this part was a narrow lane hemmed in with high hedges. The mire covered the whole of it, and I was wetted to the ankles. Cross-roads occurred frequently, and at length I thought I was going in a wrong direction judging by the position of the moon which sent a few dim rays through a cloudy atmosphere. I was on a wrong road - but at length I came to some houses and was put right. Soon after I got to an Inn, but here the beds were all occupied and they were unwilling to let me sleep in an outhouse, and wouldn't be at the trouble of preparing some supper for me. However I got directions in abundance and was told to go first to the left, and then to the right, and to hold straight up the common. As a cross-road, I went to a farm house to enquire. The door was shut. I found myself in a farmyard, and spying a cart shed went into it, and mounted a cart where I lay down. I had not been long there when I found a lift near me and got upon it. Here I found a bundle of wattlings, another of rushes, and a bit of mat and I had carried a bag with me from the cart. So I put off my napsack, and laid the bag under my head on the wattle and rushes, and spread the ragged mat over my legs, and slept, but not soundly. About midnight my feet felt very cold for they were very wet. So I put off my shoes and wrapped my feet in the mat. Wet shoes are good conductors and bad containers of caloric. The mat answered better for one foot soon got warmish, and that was enough for a strong chap like me. So I fell asleep and when I awakened today the people were up feeding the horse and the poultry.

I descended from my celestial mansion, to wade again among the mire. I felt very weak but did not experience the sensation of hunger. My hat was so crumpled that I could not get it put right, and my clothes were and are still covered with dirt of various kinds. When I had proceeded about two miles I found an Inn and entered it. Here I breakfasted upon tea, bread and butter, and eggs. But a dispute arose between the good man and the good woman about my note. They said they believed they were perfectly good, and if I had any other note, especially a Scotch one, they would readily give change, but none of the Bank of England were taken, and they chose rather to lose the shilling for my breakfast than to run the risk of taking a bad note. This was tormenting and I felt that I had done wrong in not telling them about it before I took my breakfast. The people were very kind and good-natured, and wished me not to be concerned about the matter, for said they, it is of no consequence and you are welcome to the breakfast. I am not sure but that my conduct verged upon dishonesty. However I shall not act so again. I have now gained an eminence, and have a vast prospect. Before me lies the low part of Cumberland, bounded by the Solway Firth. I can distinguish the Cathedral of Carlisle about ten or twelve miles off, but the mist has covered the Scottish hills. It is now about eleven o'clock. I write this in the open air sitting upon a tuft of grass near the road.

Keswick, Cumberland   Friday night   8th October

Till I came to Carlisle I did not perceive much difference between the dialect and that of Dumfries. After that however I found it completely altered. The English language was spoken, not indeed in purity but pretty well. I was surprised to hear thees and thous - "When thou comes to the corner" said a woman today in answer to my enquiry regarding the road, "though maun keep to the right, and when thou comes to some houses they will show thee". I thank you. "Welcome". So when I came to the houses they did show me, and soon after I wrote my last report, and then proceeded. I now passed over a long heath or common, with a pretty high hill to one side, then entered a pretty little valley, climbed an acclivity and came to a post which informed me that Carlisle was twenty miles off and Keswick nine. Here I had a fine view. In one part in the distance were lofty mountains tipped with clouds. Before me a small portion of a lake, and beyond it a cultivated plain ending in the distance in low hills. The plains of Cumberland are too much intersected by hedges and trees to appear beautiful in the landscape. Near this place I was informed that it was after two o'clock. On coming to the declivity of the hill I had a fine view of the lake. On its further side were mountains rising to a considerable height, wooded along their bases, and on the nearer a cultivated plain divided into small portions by hedges and trees ending in hills of less elevation. The lake itself was several miles in length and its margin was beautifully irregular. The road passed over the plain but at some distance from the lake and hemmed in with hedges so that for several miles I saw little of the surrounding scenery. When I had reached the middle of the lake the view improved and from there to its upper extremity I had several beautiful pieces of landscape. The lake is about six miles in length. When I got to its upper end a new scene presented a large beautiful valley appeared abounded on both sides and at the farther end by mountains. The distant mountains were low but rugged, the nearer were pretty high but smooth and in general green. In the centre of the valley flowed a large river, by which grew a good deal of wood which appeared peculiarly beautiful because differing from the hedgerows of the rest of the valley. This valley is unlike the glens of Albyn because much broader and well cultivated. The lake also is unlike the Highland lakes, having more of beauty and less of the rugged or majestic in its scenery. About its middle I washed my stockings and shoes, and the legs of my trousers in a rill, and in the dusk arrived at Keswick. This account is extremely imperfect. A dispute carried on between two fellows in the room in which I write has put the contents of my noddle into confusion.

Kendal, Westmorland   Sunday night   10th October

I am now seated in an easy chair by a large fire in the parlour of an Inn in Kendal, the chief town of Westmorland. On the other side of the fire are two fellows smoking tobacco. I applied at several inns in town before I got lodging, and I was surprised to see the number of people tippling in them. It is not so in Scotland thought I. Far different is the occupation of the Scottish tradesman and peasant on Sunday. I like not to see the Sabbath violated by people who profess the Christian religion. Today for the first time I saw it violated, and I was shocked. In one place I saw boys flying a kite, in another I met a parcel of pedlars, the bread and fruit shops were open everywhere, and on a lake I saw people sailing for pleasure. I like to see the Sabbath kept even with puritanical strictness. This may be a Scotch prejudice, not it is no prejudice, devotion of one day in seven to religious exercises is absolutely necessary to keep in mind the chief end of our existence. It serves to confirm religious habit and when the Scottish peasantry begin to think lightly of breaking the Sabbath they will become less virtuous. I would have expressed my ideas on this subject more clearly and more at length, had not two other fellows come in and raised such a clatter as to exclude the possibility of thinking unless I were deaf.

The Common Black Bryony is a new plant to me. It was common in the hedges and its large clustered berries had a beautiful appearance. Although I found no flowers I am under no doubt regarding the plant for the marks which I took on the spot of occurrence are these; planta scandeus, foliis cordatis integerrimis, caule tecti spiraliter tortus, baccis magnis rubris vel flavicantibus racemosis succosis insipidis.

Ten o'clock. I have now taken supper, and a pint of ale, and a glass of rum, and a smoke of tobacco, and have sweated out the water which I drank on the road today at a huge fire. By the bye my glass is no more - it was broken in the city of Stranraer in Scotland - and I must now bend down on my knees and hands and drink like an ox or a mule. I have got an apartment to myself too and so I begin my story and return to the town of Keswick in Northumberland, where I believe I left myself seated by a fire in the parlour or common room of an Inn with a flaming-faced fellow on the other side drinking with the landlord, and above my head a London juggler, who according to his bill could do anything with his cards but make them speak, driving like fury at a squeaking fiddle. Well, I was wet to the knees, I was fatigued, also my shoulders smarted of the straps of my napsack. I felt uncomfortable after lying half shivering and half snoring on the loft of a byre on the night before, and so after eating a supper composed principally of beef-steak, potatoes, and apple-pie, I deemed it proper and becoming and expedient to recruit my spirits and 'moistify my leather' (Burns) by taking a few drops of the creature. So I ordered a gill of rum and some warm water. "A geel of room?" asked the landlord - yes, said I, a gill of rum, why? "Because I thought it might have been a noggan!". So it came and I found that the landlord was right, and that an English gill is a Scotch half-munchkin, and verily this was a particle of knowledge gained. Many a little makes a meikle, as poor Richard says, so I fell foul of my rum and I left not 'the devil a drop' and I smoked some tobacco, and while my encephalic upper was whirling upon its axis under the twofold impulse of the spirit and the smoke I rolled myself up in the bedclothes, and fell asleep, aye and slept as 'soundly as a top'. (Goethe - Lovers Rows). The bells had tolled the ninth hour before the principle of activity had overcome the principle of laziness. At length I crawled slowly from among the blankets, like a snail out of its shell, and I put on my clothes and shaved and washed, and felt most gloriously comfortable. But, alack a day, the rains fell and the winds blew, and I was kept in the house until half past eleven. My note was changed at last, and so I left Keswick, and proceeded on the Borrodale road toward the rocks which I had observed the evening before. I had not gone far when a scene presented which called forth an involuntary exclamation indicative of wonder and delight. I climbed over some fences and got to a proper station for viewing it, and now I shall fancy myself in this very place, looking upon the scene and describing it in the present tense. Rather I shall transcribe in actual words the ideal description of this scene, as if it were delineated upon a memorandum slip of paper, laid between the leaves of the Compendium Flora Brittanica of my worthy respected friend Doctor (alias Sir J. E.) Smith of Norwich.

Monday 10 a. m. The principle objects in the landscape are a lake, an interrupted range of beautifully variegated rocks, and several lofty mountains. The lake is to appearance about three miles in length and one in breadth. It has two thickly wooded islands upon it, and its margin is finely undulated. It occupies the greater part of a plain which on one side is bounded by mountains sloping gently and in some places precipitous, on the other by lower mountains presenting the appearance of a long interrupted ridge of rocks. The mountains may be about 1500 feet above the level of the lake. Along their sides and bases they are finely wooded. No heath is seen upon them, but unless where the surface is rocky or covered with trees or brakes they are green even to their summits. At the nearer end of the range of rocky mountains on the left of the lake is a perpendicular rock upwards of a hundred feet, and at its farther end, at a distance of about four miles a number of large masses of rock with their peaks and chasms and woods blocking up the extremity of the valley. These rocky hills are all wooded excepting on the faces of the precipices, and even there a few trees are to be seen in the chinks. Along the borders of the lake, cornfields, gleaming among woods and copses are contrasted with the rugged appearance of the surrounding mountains. On one side of the lake in a beautiful spot at the base of the rocks is an elegant house, and at the further end a village is indistinctly seen. Beyond all these objects are seen in the distance lofty mountains whose summits are involved in rolling masses of dark blue vapour. A transparent mist hangs before the distant objects giving a delightful softness to the landscape. The atmosphere is cloudy but glimpses of sunshine flash through the intervals upon the rocks and woods. The colouring is soft and gently variegated from the deep shades of the chasms to the dusky hue of the distant mountains, from thence to the browns of the brakes on the hills, the green of the woods and meadows, and lastly to the yellowish tint of the stubble fields, and the light blue of the floating vapour. The surface of the lake is ruffled and the woods are waving in the breeze. Clouds are rapidly rolling along the mountain peaks. The scene is like a scene of Albyn, but I look upon it almost as I would upon a picture. Here Fingal and Oscar never strode to the hill of deer with Fillan of the fleet foot. Here the Gael of the north never dwell. Land of my youth! my heart is attached to thee, I cannot proceed. Yet although this is not Scotland, it is a part of nature, and may well call forth enthusiastic astonishment from its children. Even I, a stranger and a foreigner, look upon the scene with delight. I admire the beauty of the lake and its islands fringed with wood, and the grandeur of the surrounding mountains proceeded along the margin of the lake, and by the bases of the rocks. The woods were composed of oak, ash, holly, alder, hawthorn, birch, sycamore. At the upper end of the lake I came across two fine but small cascades tumbling from the chasms. Near one of them was an Inn with a rather odd sort of motto for a tippling house 'IN COELO QUIES'. Farther on I came to a pass among the rocks, and here was situated the village which formed part of the landscape which I have described. The rain here came on again, and the wind blew with fury from the narrow valley before me. I crossed a river by a narrow board and some stepping stones to get to the village to enquire about the road. The wind blew so hard I crossed with difficulty. However I had spite enough in me to bellow 'Blow on ye winds and crack your cheeks' (Lear). On receiving the information which I wanted I recrossed the stream and proceeded. Every turn of the road brought me to a new and beautiful scene. Among the trees which covered the bases of the hills I recognised the yew-tree which I had seen in the Botanic Garden at Edinburgh last spring. It grew here and there in the crevices of the rocks. Some miles on I came to a large block of lapis ollais standing upon an angle by the road, and near it I enquired about the road to Ambleside. I was told that in this same direction there was a sort of footpath over the fells, but that I ought to return to Keswick and take the regular road. As I am too conceited to take advice which opposes my own determination, rather as I was desirous of seeing the mountain scenery of Cumberland, I even trudged on, and soon after entered Borrowdale, a narrow valley enclosed by lofty mountains. At its upper end the road branched into two so I followed the one which leads to Ambleside. Near this place at a village I was furiously attacked by a dog, but kept him off by threats. The rain continued. I now entered an alpine valley nearly destitute of wood enclosed by green hills and terminating in a lofty mountain, on whose summit I saw the rain glistening on the face of the dark rocks. The few trees which occurred here were ash. In such a situation in Scotland they would have been birch or alder. I need not count every step which I took in ascending this long valley. Suffice it to say that I lost all traces of a footpath and that when I had got nearly to the summit of the rocky mountain the shades of night were closing around me. Few alpine plants occurred here. I saw only the Savin-leaved Club-moss, Prickly Club-moss, Common Club-moss, Fir Club-moss, and the Starry Saxifrage. At the base of the rocks on the summit of the mountain I came across a black lake, and soon after on the top of a ridge came in sight of a long valley, and saw a glimpse of a lake at a great distance. If the road went down this valley I saw that I had gone far astray. Night was falling. I saw a house in the valley and so I began to descend. However fatiguing it may be to ascend a steep mountain I have always found it more disagreeable to descend a rapid declivity, and here where the slope was composed of rocks and cairns of loose stones I proceeded but slowly. In crossing this mountain, melancholy ideas occurred several times. At one place I had before me the image of Mary MacCaskill, (*Mary was MacGillivray's aunt, the wife of his uncle Roderick*) pale and dejected, sinking under a protracted and almost hopeless disease, and I exclaimed with great vehemence "My dear Mary". At another I felt satiated with wandering - I will return, said I, to the place from whence I came, and I will study to become a useful member of society. It was a gentle and not entirely disagreeable melancholy however which I felt. Peace and harmony and universal benevolence only accorded with my ideas - and I remember distinctly to have said to myself as I approached the valley, "Poor fellow, cherish the benevolence which you now feel in your heart, and you will do well". At length I reached the bottom and soon after got onto a path. It was by this time nearly dark. The path led me to a house which I entered to enquire about the road. Here I found a young man who was soon to go about two miles down the valley, and until he should get in readiness I was desired to come in and sit down. The good woman asked if I would 'accept a bowl of warm croods'. Egash! thought I, and that I will to be sure, so I told her I should feel much obliged to her for it. And so it was set before me together with some bread, butter, and cheese. I ate the curds and a little bread. The people thought I had made a wonderful escape, and ought to be very glad that I had got over the fell before it grew dark. But I felt no great gladness on the occasion, because I thought it would be a matter of little consequence to sit under a rock all night for the weather, though wet, was very warm. Ambleside I was told was upwards of eight miles distant, but there was a public house four miles down the road. The young man took a horse from the stable and mounted it. He was accompanied by another on foot, and I followed them. The night was very dark and I could not even distinguish the stones on the road or the gates which crossed it. About two miles down the valley my companions left me. I proceeded for about a mile. I saw lights gleaming along the side of the valley but they were not from houses, being as I deemed them phosphoric. About a mile from the place where the two peasants had left me, I knocked my shin against a gate, and soon after came to a house. As the night was extremely dark I thought I could not do better than enter the house and petition for a bed in an outhouse or anywhere. When I entered I found a woman and a girl by the fire in a large neat apartment. I told them I was a stranger and had come from Keswick over the hills, and did not like to proceed further as the night was very dark, and would be obliged to them if they would allow me to sleep in an outhouse. The woman answered that she had a bed such as the family slept in, but perhaps I might not be pleased with it, as to sleeping in an outhouse, it was out of the question. So I entered and seated me by the fire. I was asked what I should like for supper. Is this an Inn asked I, somewhat surprised, no, I was answered. My supper consisted of a mess of boiled milk, beer and oatbread, crumbled, and some bread, butter, and cheese. About ten I was conducted by the good man to my bedchamber where I found an excellent bed. It was nine before I got up on Sunday morning, and I was about to offer my hostess half a crown and to depart, when she asked if I was for breakfast. I replied that I would not put her to the trouble. Come, said she, sit down, so I agreed, and tea was prepared on which, together with wheaten bread and butter I breakfasted. All this was very well, and very much I thought in the style of Highland hospitality, only that in the Highlands one is seldom asked what he chooses, this being left entirely to the discretion of the host. I clapped my baggage on my shoulders and asked my kind hostess if she would accept three shillings for her trouble. What ever you please to give Sir, answered she very readily. I gave her three shillings and thanked her for her kindness. England, thought I, thou can'st never vie with Scotland in hospitality. The wife of a Scottish farmer would never accept a bribe.

The bread which I had seen here and in other places was very thin, being only a little thicker than pasteboard, and I had deemed it wheaten. But here I was informed that it was laver-bread or oat-bread and that very little wheat was grown in the high parts of Westmorland or Cumberland. By the bye I should have mentioned that I entered the county of Westmorland somewhere about the great mountain which I crossed on Saturday. About ten I proceeded on my journey down the valley which is called Langdale. It was narrow and bounded by craggy mountains among which it winded so as to afford a new and agreeable prospect at every turn. It was well-wooded and had corn-fields and pasture grounds along the stream which ran through it. The rocks were of aluminous schists and in several places I saw slate quarries. No heath was to be seen, but bracken having now the russet hue of autumn assumed its place. About two miles from my lodging of last night I came to a small lake, not very interesting. The valley had here become broader and the mountains less majestic, and hamlets and houses appeared around. For two miles further down the scenery appeared softened, and at length turning round the base of a low hill by which there was a fine little village I got a view of Windermere, the largest of the English lakes. About half a mile further on I came to Ambleside, a pretty large village situated at the mouth of a short valley a little distance from the lake. It is romantically situated, but irregular and ill-built, the houses being of slate stones, their roofs of large nasty clay slate, and the windows composed of small panes and extremely dispropor-tioned. About twelve o'clock I proceeded on my journey. The road for some way passes along the lake, farther on it receded from it and the view is completely interrupted by trees. About four miles from Ambleside I again came in sight of the lake, and here I thought it had a slight bend, so that two distinct scenes presented, one stretching toward the north-west and west, the other to the southeast, as I judged by the position of the Sun. The first scene consisted of a part of the lake about four miles in length, narrow and winding up a broad valley enclosed by low hills. In all this course were cornfields, pastures, woods and villages beautifully intermixed. In the distance appeared lofty mountains with their peaks and ridges tipped with dusky clouds. The other scene consisted of a larger proportion of the same lake winding down a long valley bounded by low wooded hills. No alpine scenery appeared in this direction, but the margin of the lake was beautifully irregular forming bays and capes. The valley was wooded so that little cultivated land appeared. On the lake were two islands, and along its banks gentleman's seats embowered among the trees. About a mile farther on I left the lake and proceeded along a rugged tract covered with heath and rocks, with cornfields and woods scattered here and there, for eight miles until I reached Kendal, situated in a rich valley, about five o'clock. The trees were of the following species; oak, ash, hazel, holly, mountain ash, hawthorn, sloe-berry, and some of the following which appeared cultivated, fir, spruce, larch, chestnut, yew.

Horsley.
'even sad vicissitude amused his soul' Beattie.
Last night I slept on the clay floor of an outhouse among cow dung without a culm of straw. Tonight I am comfortably seated in the parlour of an Inn and will probably sleep in a bed. Yesterday I was employed in writing till about 2 o'clock. Till this time alas it rained, so that I could not have proceeded however. When about to depart I looked for my hat where I had left it in the parlour, but lo, it was not there, nor could it be found in the house. 'Experience teaches fools' as the saying is, and I dare say I shall not leave my hat or my wig either, among a parcel of drunken sots in an English Inn, especially on a Sunday night. The

circumstance did not affect me in the least and I went to a hatters and got a substitute for seven shillings and sixpence. So I marched along leaving the town about half past two. By the bye, previously to setting out I had a dispute with a drunken carter who wanted me to ride with him for part of the way. The insolence of this sot irritated me and I told him to get about his business. He called me proud and saucy and so on but still persisted in his importunities, and by the way he kept tormenting me for some time. It was six o'clock when I reached Burton but I felt fresh and was anxious to proceed, and proceed I did splashing through the mire until the tenth milestone from Burton. There had been a great fair at Lancaster and I felt assured in consequence that I should not get a bed, and being desirous to see the town thought proper to search for a sheltered place in the neighbourhood. I got over a wall and searched around for some time, till after wandering among the fields about half a mile I fell upon a large, mis-shapen house with a two-folding door or gate. It was by this time about ten o'clock and the moon was up, but the sky being cloudy it was dark. I entered the house and groped about until I had made a complete circuit and arrived at the door from which I had begun. No straw was to be felt and there was not a loft. The floor was soft and damp. However I felt it more comfortable than a hedge side which I had tried some time before, and so put off my napsack and hat, and tied a handkerchief around my head, and extended me on the floor by the wall just behind the door. My feet were wet yet I did not shiver in the least as the night was warm, and I slept tolerably till about midnight or rather after it, when I arose and took a peep at the moon and walked up and down the floor for a short time. I then lay down and put my head on my napsack as before and fell asleep. When I awakened about sunrise I found myself on the banks of a beautiful river with the city of Lancaster and its superb castle about half a mile distant. I washed my face in the river and proceeded on my journey.

Manchester   Wednesday 13th October   Evening

Evil communication corrupts good manners as St Paul observes. It is a noble religion. Surely, surely it is not of human invention. I should be sorry was I convinced that it were. Its principles are those which I acknowledge as the only true principles and I endeavour to render my practice conformable to its precepts. Doubts arise only respecting its origin. Surely such a noble religion could not be the production of human invention, yet, as I have said doubts occur. To return to the remark of the great apostle of the gentiles, I am so much influenced by the examples of those around me that on entering an Inn in the evening I call for a pipe and a pint of ale. The very pronunciation of the people I involuntarily ape and nowhere since I entered England have I been taken for a Scotchman excepting here tonight. Twice indeed I have been thought an Irishman, but in general I think I have reason to believe that I am considered as an Englishman. On entering this great city I applied at several places for lodging but was refused. In the house in which I now am I was at first told that all the beds were engaged, but there was a hesitation in the affirmation of the landlady which led me to think that she told a lie, and I was right. So a conversation ensued which ended in my admittance. As I was walking along the streets I thought that I was dogged by a thin ill-looking fellow. I turned about and stood as if I were waiting some person. "Sir" said the fellow as if I had spoken to him. I said nothing. "Do you know me?" asked he. No, I do not, answered I, impressingly, perhaps surlily. "Upon my word, I beg your pardon" said he "I thought your name had been John Parkins".

Today I saw a horrid face, the worst I believe which I have ever seen. It was that of a half-drunk pedestrian whom I passed on the road. He asked if I was going far, a little way, answered I. Have you any news - nothing in particular. I accelerated my pace and soon left him out of sight. Lavater, thou art right! There is as necessary a connection between the corporeal and mental frame as there is between cause and effect. This is in fact, cause and effect, but this leads to a theory which I must defer. If there be a 'human face divine' (Milton) there is also a human face demonical and the very sight of the Devil himself, if there really be such an animal could scarcely produce more horror and repugnance in me than that of the fellow bearing his image whom I saw today. The stamp of innocence cannot be mistaken, that of vice may, physiognomy is a noble study but who can detect the truth with certainty? Who but the searcher of hearts can trace events to their primary causes? I have some idea of the rapture which Lavater experienced on seeing the marks of virtue impressed on the countenance, yes, I have experienced it myself. Dear objects of my admiration, your images are impressed on my heart. Beauty without these marks is nothing in my eye, they give amiableness even to deformity.

Yesterday on getting up from my clay-cold bed I washed my face in the river, as has been said, and proceeded on my journey. I ate a pennyworth of bread, and soon after drank a pint of ale. The day was warm without a breath of wind. I passed through the city of Lancaster where as I have said a great fair was then kept. The people were busy erecting their stalls and for some miles from the town the road was crowded with people and carts. Before night I was weary, and sick at heart, not that I was unwell, in so far as regarded my corporeal mechanism, but I passed over such a desert of cultivated fields, hedges and villages, and everything was so uninteresting that the remembrance of the scenery of Scotia came to my mind associated with a thousand agreeable images whose contrast excited melancholy and extreme impatience, and I had almost determined to take a seat in a stage coach to finish my journey in a hurry. Farewell Flora, and farewell Fauna, said I as I descended the mountains of Westmorland. I had not now therefore the company of these my favourites. I was out of trim too; my trowsers are ragged and are as nicely plastered with mire as the clay cottages of Cumberland, my shoes are nearly worn done, and my stockings are fairly finished. The roads were bad and muddy, and the weather was warm even to the extreme. But when I reached Chorley and got seated by a blazing fire, and smoked a pipe and supped, my spirits returned, and I thought I should walk to London although my stumps should be worn off to the knees. Yesterday I walked thirty one miles and as my shoes were bad my feet were very sore, and one of them a little cut. I got an excellent bed and as I was crawling into it and felt it so luxuriously soft I contrasted it with my bed of the former night and felt a degree of pleasure which I had scarcely thought a bed, considered in its own simple capacity, could yield. Without pain there could not be pleasure. But whether there be an absolute pleasure as there is absolute and irrelative beauty I do not know. If pain and pleasure, deformity and beauty be more relative ideas, it will follow that vice and virtue are the same. I am not willing to allow this however, yet I may be wrong. I was a little amused with the John Bull figures of the farmers about Lancaster, such vast lumps of tallow. If a parcel of them were set upon the top of Ben Nevis what glorious fun it would be to see them coming down, but as to their climbing up the mountain, that is quite out of the question. I met one of these animals near the town of Garstang between Lancaster and Preston, and was admiring the shortness of his legs, when it remarked that I was in a great hurry. I was walking at the rate of three miles in the hour quite composedly but he was sweating and puffing away at about half a mile in the hour. What? said I. You are in a great hurry, said he - no I am not, said I - aren't you - No. I was a little irritated by the impudence of the thing. "Where have you come from?" "From the North". "Is there any quarreling there? Any fighting?" No. "From what part of the North have you come?" from Scotland. So I began to walk on. "Where are you going?" To London. 'Aye' - said he, expressing disbelief in a very vulgar manner 'very likely'. What have you to do with that? asked I. My Scotch blood was beginning to move with great rapidity by this time, and I wheeled about and was proceeding on my journey. "You are a very clever young fellow" said he, "I dare say you have some good business on hand". Yes, I have, said I, turning again - what have you to do with my business. What right have you to ask about it. Let me hear no more such impertinent questions. "Oh, no right at all" muttered the fellow sneaking away "Farewell, farewell, good morrow, good morrow". Today I rose about nine. It was half past ten before I set off. The weather was fine and there was a slight breeze. I travelled twenty two miles and got here before dark. Halfway between this place and Chorley I passed through the town of Bolton. Between Preston and this the towns are filled with cotton manufacturers, and even along the roads I heard the noise of looms every now and then. The whole of Lancashire through which I have passed is very plain, or rather composed of little eminences and depressions. Few places appeared uncultivated and these only the tops of hills. About four miles on this side of Bolton where the road passes over an eminence the view is very extensive over a plain country. In the southwest I saw the hills of Flintshire or perhaps Cheshire with the mouth of the Mersey, and in the south east in the middle of a vast plain, the city of Manchester.

Buxton, Derbyshire   Friday 15th October   10 a. m.
'England, with all thy faults, I love thee still' (Cowper).

Get thee behind me, Scotland, said I last evening as I began to ascend the hills of Derbyshire. I had passed the plains of Lancashire with its ugly brick-built towns, and was entering upon a hilly country where the whole surface was not occupied with cornfields and hedges. Deep wooded vallies, rivers, cottages, churches, and villages built of stone, tracts of heath covered with plantations now occurred, and I again felt cheerful. About ten o'clock yesterday I left Manchester, and such an abominable dunghill of a town I never before saw. Narrow, irregular, dirty streets, misshapen brick houses daubed over with paint and whitening. Hideous manufactories with their sooty smoke-disgorging chimneys towering amongst the pestilential clouds that rolled over the city - crowds of ill-looking and deformed raggamuffins, waggons laden with coal and beer butts, the intolerable stench arising from tallow chandleries, tanneries, sewers, and butchers stalls, etc, etc. The skirts of the city are however not so bad. Here the streets are wide, and the houses large and regular. On getting onto the London road my spirits revived. The sight of a stone marked with 'To London 182 miles' inspired me with fresh vigour, and for sometime I trudged along as cheerily as if I had been within three hours march of the great city, the goal at which my wild goose chase is to terminate. I now entered Cheshire, and seven miles from Manchester passed through the town of Stockport. For several miles farther the country was still plain but as I approached Derbyshire the scenery improved. Green hills and large beautiful vallies occurred and the prospect became more extensive, and thus it continued until I began to ascend the hills of Derbyshire, when I even became so cheerful as to whistle a tune, and to utter the expression with which this report commences. Yesterday I walked only twenty four miles. London is still distant one hundred and fifty eight miles. I propose to be there on Thursday at about two o'clock, that is at the rate of twenty six miles a day. Ten shillings and sixpence is the sum to be expended on this part of my journey, that is one and twenty pence a day. I thought to have travelled more cheaply than I do, but I find it needless to torment myself with bad meals when there is no occasion. If there were necessity for it I know by experience that I can bear hunger as well as most people but as there is not, I will even indulge my gluttonous appetite so far as to live upon about one third of what the generality of travellers placed exactly in my circumstances, excepting in regard to the article pecunia, would expend, and would think little enough. I once travelled two hundred and forty miles upon twelve shillings, on the other hand I have spent fifteen shillings in one day on my travels. These are my extremes. The breakfasts which they give in the middling sort of Inns in England are miserable. About half a dozen of slices of bread almost as thin as the laver-meal scones of Cumberland, that is as thin as paste board, covered with salt butter, and three cups of tea or coffee, nothing more, no egg, no beef, no bacon, no fish. The reason I believe is that the dinner hour is twelve o'clock. In Scotland it is quite different. The breakfast must be   substantial because the hour of dinner is placed at the other end of the day. In the Highlands for instance, the tacksmen have tea or coffee, oat or barley bread (commonly both), fresh and salt butter, eggs, fish, and potatoes, and cheese. Cold beef or mutton is sometimes substituted for the fish, but the potatoes and the cheese are never dispensed with, excepting in a few places where they are beginning to ape the Saxons. Dr Johnson tells us very gravely that wherever he would sup he would certainly breakfast in Scotland. The Highlanders make breakfast the most substantial and supper the lightest meal, the English reverse this order. That the good sense of the Highlanders is superior in regard to this, every unprejudiced person who has common sense will readily assert.

Lough-borough Leicestershire Sunday

I have advanced fifty miles since writing my last report so that I am now within a hundred and ten miles of the great city of the South. On Friday at twelve o'clock I left Buxton which is a watering place situated on the northwest of Derbyshire. Jupiter and Flora both smiled benignantly upon me. The weather was so fine that the larks were singing as in an April morning, and I had not proceeded a quarter of a mile when I observed an unknown plant. It proved to be the Musk Thistle *Carduus nutans*, the most beautiful thistle which I have yet seen, so instead of *Carduus nutans* which occurs in my lists, the Welted Thistle *Carduus acanthoides*, must be read. Although one may commit little mistakes in Botany, it is pleasant to feel assured that he can rectify them by his own observation, without the assistance of others. Soon after I found another plant, the Common Carline Thistle. Everything conspired to render me cheerful; the serenity of the weather, the agreeable keeness of the air, the finding of these plants, and the feeling of perfect health and freshness, but above all the wideness of the prospect, and the change in the nature of the country over which I passed. For about fifteen miles from Buxton the country is hilly and bare, consisting chiefly of pasture ground, enclosed by stone fences, without trees or hedges. It is not absolutely sterile but compared with Lancashire it might be called so. The contrast however, between the counties, afforded me pleasure. I had been sick to

117

the soul of travelling over the low fertile plains of Lancashire and Cheshire when the view was in many places confined to the road and the houses which bordered it. But here the view was not limited by hedges and trees, and I saw on both sides to the distance of thirty miles and more. The idea of liberty was associated with the appearance of the country and my heart bounded with gladness. The hills did not in any place rise to a considerable height, and the absence of a sylvan verdure and the dull sameness of the grey stone fences might have made me in certain circumstances to pronounce the country disagreeable, but at the time I thought it delightful. When I had proceeded about sixteen miles I found the country changed. I was now descending from the hills and entering upon a low district. Four miles farther I reached the town of Ashbourne about seven o'clock. The birds which I observed on the high part of Derbyshire were the following: Skylark, Rook, Starling, Hedge Sparrow, Pied Wagtail, Wren, Chaffinch, Magpie, and Yellow-hammer. On reaching Ashbourne I went into a shop and bought some cheese, for as my money was scarce I had half resolved to sleep out all night since the weather was not cold. It was dark by this time. I proceeded along a spell and found that I had gone out of the London road. I was directed to it however and on finding it went into a shop to buy some bread. A girl asked if I had got a bed. No, I said, have you beds? Yes, so I understood it was a lodging house for pedlars and poor stragglers such as abound in Galloway and are intended for the reception of Irish vagrants. And so, I entered the kitchen or parlour for I know how cheap boarding and lodging are in such houses and I expected some fun. The company at suppertime consisted of Irish pedlars, an Italian picture and looking glass vendor, a Don-Quixote shoremaker who spoke not a word, the landlord and landlady, a couple of spindle-shanked, lantern-jawed creatures, two young girls, and a fat bull-dog (or bull-bitch) looking woman whose tongue moved with the volubility of a thresher's flair. In houses of this sort there is no common table, but every person gets what he chooses and eats it by himself. The articles are furnished by the people of the house, and in general no charge is made for the trouble of preparing them. Here there was a kettle boiling on the fire. One of the Irishmen who had a face like an ape's, with a mouth from the middle of one cheek to the same place on the other first fell to work. He got a teapot and cup and a loaf and fell to work on one side of a large table. The Italian boy who had a finely formed face, followed his example.

When they had done, the second Irishman took out of his pocket an earthen-ware bottle, and took some tea from it. He brought a large loaf from the shop, and a pennyworth of butter and set his masticators in motion. I could not refuse to follow the example of people so worthy of imitation. Besides my stomach was grumbling for it said that the feeling supplied by the four cups of tea and two slices of toast which I had eaten in the morning had long ago been expended. Well, I went to the shop and got three-halfpence worth of tea and a pennyworth of sugar, a pennyworth of apples, and a pipe of tobacco, and seating me on a long sofa by the table, between the Irishman and the Italian, laid my stores upon the table, and extricated from the folds of a handkerchief a loaf and half a pound of Cheshire cheese. Well, I protest I supped more heartily and more contentedly than I had done for weeks before, and then I had a glorious fumigation from a long-stalked pipe, and ate some apples. Meanwhile the Irishmen and I had become very gracious. I told them the Irish and the Scotch Highlanders were one and the same people, and we compared the languages and lo! they were found to be the same, to the great delight of the little ape-faced fellow, who appeared very much pleased with the distinctness of my pronounciation, for he said, the English muttered their words so indistinctly that he could scarcely understand them. I asked the Italian if he longed to get home. No, said he, I like England better than Italy. This is very strange thought I, for I am sure I should never like it better than Scotland. I have not time at present to proceed with my narrative, but rather than omit it altogether I shall transcribe the notes which I wrote on a slip of paper in my bedchamber that same night.

The Irishmen and I had a great number of fine stories about football, shinnie, (*shinty*) and funerals in a smoky kitchen parlour with a large table, a sort of sofa, and a tea-making kettle. Two young women favoured us with their company for some time, but they used unmannerly words. I don't care much to hear them with black-guardish Irish pedlars but I am horror struck when young women curse and utter obscene language. I felt at first great repugnance to mingling with the beasts but my apprehensions soon vanished. The Irishmen talked more rationally than I thought they could and were mightily civil, but the English were - humph - so and so - One of the girls had a tongue like -- la! What volubility! Let me home again to Scotland, thought I, among a parcel of islanders I would be quite happy, aye, and among a parcel of lowlanders too. There, there would be the attraction of cohesion, but here there is nothing but electric repulsion. I smoked a penn'orth of tobacco, and ascended two pair of stairs with my Irishmen. One of them showed me to my bed. "Goodnight, Sir". "Goodnight". Three beds. In one was the poor Italian boy. He has a good face. I felt attached to him because he was a stranger and I could not help looking often at him. At length I got seated beside him. I asked the Italian of several things mentioning at the same time the Latin for them, and there was a great resemblance. He did not mix with the people, but looked like a lamb among wolves, or a lap-dog among terriers. I wish I had the gas lights of Glasgow to set them aburning all night. My napsack shall lie under my head. A good light and fair play, I care no deils aboddle, but in truth I would rather encounter auld clootie* than a parcel of Irish tinkers.

Past ten o'clock

I got a good bed and slept soundly. Yesterday morning I rose before eight; the Irishmen were getting their breakfast ready. I got a pennyworth of tea, a pennyworth of sugar, and two pence worth of bread, and breakfasted very contentedly. I then sallied forth. The weather was delightful. Two miles from Ashbourn I found the Musk Mallow in flower. I had seen it at Dumbarton and examined it there, but not methodically as it was out of flower. Further on I found a shrew-mouse lying on the road. About three miles from town I found the Ivy-leaved Toad-flax growing on a bridge. This species I had examined in the Botanic Garden at Glasgow. I reached the town of Derby between twelve and one, and purchased some bread and cheese which I dined on in a field. Derby is a small town. The houses in it and in Ashbourn are built of brick. About eight miles farther on I entered the county of Leicester and soon after came to the town of Kegworth. Near it I found a plant I had not seen before. It is a Teasel but I am not quite sure whether it is the Fuller's Teasel D. fullonum or the Wild Teasel D. sylvestris. It grew by hedges in moist places. It has these characters; D. foliis connatus, serratis, caule foliis que aculeato, paleis spinosis porresta, recurvatis, involucrie deflexo, incurvatis, capitule longioribus. Planta tri-ves, quadripedalis. Near Derby I also found and examined the Common Meliflot, a plant of which I had seen a garden specimen in Aberdeen which had defied me, and which Convenor Rannie of the Old Town had named the Tonkay bean plant, from the

* Robert Burns, *Address to the Deil*.

similarity of its smell to that of the fruit! This plant occurred about three miles south of Derby. To the north of it I found the Water Figwort which I examined after dining. It was seven o'clock before I arrived here. One of the Irishmen of Ashbourn had directed me to a Mr or Mrs Brewin. I found one of that name here, but he proved to be a Constable and not an Innkeeper, so we conjectured it to have been a joke. However I found a good Inn and was well treated, and if I had a little more money I should remain here tonight, but I believe I must be off. And off I went accordingly but not till I had eaten a good dinner with the Landlord and Landlady, and had drunk a cup of ale. About three o'clock I left Loughborough and proceeded cheerily along a good road. The weather was fine with an exhilarating tinge of frost in the air. I observed vines in several places nailed up to the walls of the houses. The grapes ripened in the open air, but were small. Within two or three miles of the town I found and examined the Field Mouse-ear Chick-weed, Black Horehound, and Common Creeping Cinque-foil. About five miles on I saw a little green bird by a streamlet which I supposed to be the Kingfisher. In the dusk I passed through Leicester, the head town of the county of that name. It appeared to be about the size of Aberdeen. As I travelled along I was delighted by the sight of the Aurora borealis gleaming among some dark clouds in the north. I felt uncommonly cheerful and fresh and proceeded four or five miles farther, in all fifteen or sixteen. The sky became suddenly overcast and rain began to fall. A barnyard with some large stacks appeared irresistibly inviting and so I clambered over the fence and sat down by a stack where I amused me for some time with picking oats. I then rose and searched for a convenient dormitory, at length I found a heap of straw, and making a hole in it, entered and lay down with my napsack under my head and a handkerchief about it. The night was very cold and the wind blew through the straw so that I could not sleep. About midnight I rose and gathered more straw about me, but it would not do. There is a degree of cold which effectually prevents sleep. The sky was clear and the keeness of the air indicated frost, so about two or three o'clock I got up and continued my journey. I met several people but nobody molested me. When the sun began to appear I found myself at the 80th milestone from London. I felt weak and my feet were sore, for the road was extremely hard. The grass was white with frost, and I was obliged to keep my hands in my pockets for I had lost my gloves about three weeks before. About eight o'clock I got some bread in a village and lay down by a haystack to eat it. Here I cut my thumb, I believe to the bone. The weather soon after grew warmer, but I grew more tired, so that it was two o'clock when I reached Northampton. Here I dined by a dyke on two pence worth of bread and two pence worth of cheese, and then entered an alehouse where I drank a cup and smoked a pipe and read a piece of a newspaper. Near this town I met four fellows on the road. On seeing me approach one of them kneeled down in the middle of the road and began playing tricks with a bullet and three cups. He appeared to have had a dispute with one of his companions and laid a wager of a shilling with him. This he lost. O'll wager a pound note, said he, again moving the cups rapidly and placing one on the ground, that the ball is under this cup. Done, said one of his companions. The ball had rolled away and another fellow took it up. I stood a little to see how it would terminate. Will you hold this note, said one of the fellows to me, taking out a bit of paper all crumpled. "Not I" said I marching along, "I don't care about it". "Damned stupid fellow" muttered the juggler "you've lost it". Ah ha my friend, thought I, you shan't hoax me, and proceeded upon my journey.

London   Thursday 21st October   10. 00 a. m.

I was prevented from finishing my story by the grumbling of an old suspicious hag of a landlady who would not have a candle burning all night in her house, that she wouldn't. Near Northampton I found specimens of the Common Night-shade, Greater Knapweed, Dwarf Mallow, which I examined soon after leaving the town. Flora still continued to smile upon me and in the evening I found the Common Traveller's Joy which I examined in the Inn. The Inn at which I staid is in a village called Grafton Regis between Northampton and Stoney Stratford, and fifty eight miles from London, so that I had walked fifty one miles without sleeping. I supped upon cold meat and bread and a cup of ale, and after smoking a pipe and writing a little, got into bed. My bed was good, and I slept very soundly as may be supposed. Let any fellow who wishes to feel what it is to sleep soundly walk fifty miles upon a very hard road and stay out a night in frosty weather, and then roll himself among some warm blankets, and he will feel it. On Tuesday I rose about nine. My money was now reduced to thirteen pence halfpenny, and I was still sixty miles from

London, excepting two. So I could not get breakfast, and left the Inn without eating anything. At a village some miles on I got a twopenny cake, and at Stratford a penny worth of gingerbread, and a pennyworth of apples, and trudged along. The weather was very fine, but the road was very hard, and my shoes and stockings quite in tatters, so that the gravel was getting in and tormenting me. Nothing interesting occurred through the day. In the dusk I passed through Dunstable, where I stood for some time unable to determine whether I should proceed or step into an Inn. What is the use of making resolutions, said I, if I cannot keep them. I went into a shop to get some bread and proceeded. About midnight I passed through the town of St Albans in Hartfordshire. Three miles farther on I grew tired and went into a park where I lay down under a large tree. Here I remained about four hours. At length I heard cocks crowing and a herd of oxen on the road, and got up. But I felt weak and my feet were excessively sore. The weather had changed and it now rained pretty hard. I was however within eighteen miles of London and had still threepence halfpenny in my pocket. So I got bread and an apple with my copper clinkum and crawled along. The rain continued. At the end of every two or three miles I was obliged to sit down to ease my feet. At length I got to Highgate about twelve o'clock and soon after entered London. The rain poured down in torrents and I was wetted to the skin. A bundle which I had directed to be sent me from Aberdeen was addressed to a Mr Cowie, a bookseller, No 31 Poultry. So I managed though with great difficulty to crawl there. My parcel had arrived and in it I found a letter from the Isles from Mary MacCaskill. This however did not ease my feet which were intolerably sore and I was obliged to stand for several hours waiting for a servant of Mr Cowie's who was to procure lodging for me. Mr Cowie is a Scotchman from Banff. I was directed to him by Dr Barclay. He was very kind and affable and I dined with him. At length a room was got for me and I proceeded to it with my baggage. After washing my feet with warm water I got into a famous bed and had a glorious snoring bout until nine this morning, when I arose and breakfasted. I have now got into decent clothes, and I had need as may readily be believed after performing a journey of eight hundred miles on foot.

Thursday evening.

I forgot to mention in its proper place that I had examined on Tuesday the Blue Bramble Rubus caesius. It occurred in several places by the road, and I eat a great quantity of its berries which I found delicious and quite unlike those of the Common Bramble Rubus fruticosus which are almost nauseous. Yesterday I found and examined another plant by the road near the fifteenth milestone, the Wild Succory. The Small Bindweed I found very common, but it is out of flower. I have now finished my journey and I am satisfied with my conduct. It is not every young man who would readily undertake to walk eight hundred miles, and very few who would accomplish such an undertaking, under the provoking allurement of every now and then falling in with a stage coach that might carry them to the end of their journey in a very short time and with less expense than if they walked. Once indeed I was very nearly lost, that is my resolution was nearly overcome, and I had almost determined when at Manchester to take a seat. But I knew that I would have repented this for years and I persisted and I am glad of it. When at Buxton it may be remembered I determined to be at London on Thursday by twelve o'clock and to spend only ten shillings and sixpence, and this too I accomplished, for I got here a day before the time, and did not expend more money than the sum mentioned. This was not effected without some painful effort. It cost me the lack of sleep for two nights, and obliged me to travel at one stretch 51 and at another 58 miles, and to live a day upon bread and water. But I consider these as very trifling hardships compared with those which I might undergo on a serious journey, to the interior of Africa, for instance, or to China by Tartary, and I am now glad that I kept my resolution. With a sufficient motive, and an alluring object in view I would undertake to travel to the uttermost corner of the earth. England is certainly a very fine country, but I would not live in it. I have already spoken of Cumberland, Westmorland, Lancashire, Cheshire, and the high part of Derbyshire. The other counties over which I have passed are Leicestershire, Northamptonshire, Buckinghamshire, Bedfordshire, Hartfordshire, and Middlesex. In all these the appearance of the country is the same. There are hills, yet the surface is not flat but rising gently here and there so as to give in many places extensive prospects. In the course which I took I did not see an acre of ground uncultivated. The whole country was laid out in fields, in some places large, in others small, enclosed by thorn fences adorned with rows of oaks and elms. Sometimes a few trees were to be seen in the fields but in general they were confined to the hedges. The most common tree is the Oak, and next to it, the Elm and the Ash. The trees are not so large as I expected and I saw none exceeding three and a half feet in diameter. I was exceedingly displeased with the mode in which the Elms are treated. The branches are lopped off close to the ground to within about fifteen feet of the summit. Small twigs are thus produced all along the stem which gives the tree a very odd appearance. The hedge rows of trees cropped in this style form a prominent feature in the English landscape. Towns and villages I found pretty numerous. The houses are not of the finest, and are generally of brick. The abodes of the peasantry are perhaps superior to those in Scotland but they are not so neat as in the southern part of that Kingdom. They are built in such a droll and disproportionate style that they often excited merriment. Nowhere have I seen houses equal to those of the peasantry in Clydesdale. The people are in general well formed, rather they were just tolerable. In Cumberland, Westmorland, and Derbyshire they were superior to those in the other counties. In Lancashire the vast unwieldy masses of corruption appeared of whom I have spoken. But nowhere else did I find many corpulent people. I had been led to believe that the English peasantry had disproportionately small legs, but this is not the case in the counties through which I have passed. The women are like the men, tolerable. A few very beautiful specimens occurred. I saw one exquisitely beautiful young lady in Kendal. If that girl, thought I were placed in the city of Glasgow, she would have as great a stream of admirers about her as a candle has of moths in a summer night. The English women are smarter and more cleanly than the Scotch. They do not strike me as peculiarly beautiful, I rather deem them below the middling order. There is not a national peculiarity to be traced among them. Faces occur of every kind, bulldog, fox, ape, ox and ass faces, and some of an opposite description. The general colours of the hair are black, brown and fair, very few red occurred. The English have been represented as an unsocial people. I found them otherwise. I speak of course only of the lower orders. The small Inns by the way I generally found crowded with ale drinkers who were commonly pretty social and merry. It is amusing to look upon a roomful of these fellows, divided into small groups each having his jug before him, and his pipe in his mouth, but ah! how unlike are they in point of sociality to a parcel of Highlanders around a reeking bowl of punch. One Highlander has as much of sociality and affection in him as a score of Englishmen.

I am just smoking a Maryland Cigar. I would recommend to travellers to learn to smoke tobacco. It is amusing and pleasing when after a hard day's walk one gets seated by a blazing ingle, to get himself enveloped in a cloud of smoke. I learned to smoke in the Isle of Harris and to snuff in Aberdeen, and I have been much addicted to both practices. But I have not allowed them to form a habit. To prevent this I have often intermitted them for weeks and months. Last winter I snuffed a great deal but I gave up the practice about two months ago, it is a dirty one. I had not smoked for upwards of a year before till I entered England about a fortnight ago, and now I am keen upon it. I like to exercise my resolution in renouncing bad habits, and I am pleased with my success. I shall soon give up smoking. A sentence in The Economy of Human Life is continually in my mind 'It is their glory to combat evil habits'. What a queer sort of dream this journey of mine has been, I laugh when I think of it. Bein-na-buird, Cairngorm, Kirk-alloway, the grave of Burns, the fells of Westmorland, Lancashire, and the frosty night among the straw. Odds splutterkins! I must have a scamper in America or Switzerland and see a little of this world of ours, and then I shall sit down by my own fireside with my ---- on one side of me and a parcel of curly headed raggamuffins on the other, and two or three friends, and we shall have a reeking cann and a glorious fumigation, and I shall read my stories and tell my jokes, and we shall slip slowly and cheerily down the vale of years, and drop into the grave. And someone may shed a tear over us, as I did over poor Burns, and we shall all in the lapse of ages be forgotten, but we shall live in a happier world, or if in a worse, God's will be done - Amen.

London   Friday 22 October   8 pm

One great spirit of animation pervades the whole Universe, producing different effects or phenomena according to the nature and structure of the bodies on which it operates. In organised bodies it produces sensation and the motions by which the functions necessary for existence are performed. That is, when it falls in with a body capable of life, it animates it. Hence could a machine be made by human art which could perform the functions necessary for life, even for an hour or shorter period of time, this machine would undoubtedly receive the primary and essential impulse from the pervading principle of life. When the organs of the animal machine are worn out, or otherwise incapacitated from performing their functions, the principle forsakes them and they then become subservient to the laws by which inorganic matter is regulated. The animating principle of a man is the same as that of a horse, an insect, or a worm. The difference in instinct or reason depends entirely upon the material structure of these different animals. A man has more sagacity merely because his organs are better adapted to its exercise. A horse with the wisdom of a man would be miserable, a man with the knowledge of a lobster and no more would be an absurdity. In the first case there would be knowledge without the power of exercising it, in the other there would be the means of exercising knowledge without the power. Nature produces no such beings. The degree of knowledge or instinct is exactly suited to the animal in the scale of existence. A man has reason because he has organs adapted to its exercise. The superiority of one man over another in particular points depends entirely upon the better conformation of his organs. Is a man noted for his strength, and is it not because his bones are large, and his muscles brawny and firm? The acumen of every faculty depends upon the temperament of the body, again, a man naturally irrascible could not possibly have been dull and heavy, and a man of coarse organisation can never be made to make nice discriminations, or acquire a fine taste. The lion lives by rapine simply because his organs are formed for such a life. The ox eats grass because he is too unwieldy to catch prey, and because although he could, his teeth are not formed for tearing flesh, nor his stomachs for digesting it. How could a tiger eat grass? How could a paradise of peace have existed if the animals which we now have were created at the beginning of the world? How could the lion lie down with the lamb, or sport with the fawn? And how could the serpent have been doomed to crawl along the ground when it is evident his form incapacitated him from any other permanent posture? Moses, Moses! I am afraid thou wilt one day be placed with Mahomet, side by side. Pray Mr Gesner, (Death of Abel) upon what did the hawk live before it learned to kill pigeons after the expulsion of Adam and Eve? Was it upon grass, figs, cherries, or cocoa nuts? Story-tellers would require more ingenuity than they commonly have, yea, more than even Dean Swift had, and William MacGillivray require to let his judgement maturate before he presumed to ridicule such an awful animal as Moses, ergo let me change the topic.

I have been strolling through the city and peeping everywhere. I went in at a door to look at some statues and a fellow put me out by the shoulders, very gently though. I have been upon two of the bridges and on the gallery of the Monument, and I have perambulated some scores of streets. And what is this great city to me - I would rather be enthroned among clouds on the peaks of Chimborago. I went to see the menagerie at Exeter Change. I was disappointed, completely disappointed. How different is this lion thought I from what he would be on the wilds of Africa? I shall never relish the study of Nature other than from the book of Nature direct. There was a poor little beautiful creature of the deer genus with an amputated leg, and the sight of it spoiled the whole. However I laughed at the hopping of a kangaroo, and the running of two gigantic cranes 7 feet in height through the room, and I peeped at the elephant like a mouse peeping at a cat. I paid my three shillings and came away quite disappointed - I had seen the animals before. I can make an excursion of four or five miles through the city and find my way back again well enough. But it is not easy for a stranger to ascertain his latitude in the streets of London, and today as I was returning from the Tower, I unwittingly made a circumbendibus of a mile or two and at last found myself at the very place from which I had set out. And then such crowds of dandies! And if you run across a street you are in danger of being trodden down by horses, and if you get into a crowd you must feel your coat tails every now and then to see that the light fingered gentry have not run off with them. I have not the good fortune however to be surprised at anything I see - only the first sight of St Pauls made me bless my stars, and the second and the third had the same effect. I like the Monument too - there is a fine view of the city from it, but the smoke prevents one from seeing very far. The spiral stair of the Monument I dare say is the longest in Britain, it has 322 steps. I counted them as I descended slowly and solitarily. A Jew I am told threw himself down from it some years ago. Egash! think I, he must have had more courage than I could muster, and if I were for a journey to my long home, I would even content me with sending a pistol bullet through my empty noddle. I should have no poisoning, no hanging, no drowning, no bleeding, - nothing but an explosion, and off in a moment to Beelzebub. But to throw myself from a rock, I almost shudder at the idea of it, and yet Miss Sappho took such a leap once. I hate of all things to tumble down a precipice. I do remember me upon a raw and gusty day when I had clambered up the rock of Dunottar Castle, simply because I could not condescend to ask admittance by the gate of Dr Young, and then began to look down from the top of the rock, that I could not venture to return, and so I tried to break the lock of the gate, but could not, and attempted another passage down the rock but was forced to return. The very idea of being on the brink of a precipice made my legs tremble. So I thought what I should do - and I determined to proceed to work quite composedly and resolutely, and thus I got down with almost as little fear as if I had been descending from the Monument of London. I do remember also that when in the Isle of Harris I had clambered to the overhanging angle of a precipice four hundred feet above the sea with a heavy musket in order to shoot at an eagle upon her nest. My head grew dizzy, and had not our shepherd come to my assistance I had been obliged to remain there all night. Goodnight Miss, Mrs, or Mr Reader.

London   Saturday 2nd October   10 pm

Yesterday it was very cold and a great deal of snow had fallen under night. Today the weather was fine. I did not get out until about twelve o'clock. I had carried with me a letter of introduction to a Mr Ogilvie from Aberdeen which Mr Shand had given me, and Dr Ewing had sent me another to Mr Brookes the anatomist. So I went in search of these gentlemen, and found them. Mr Ogilvie was 'particularly engaged' but desired me to breakfast with him on Tuesday. Mr Brookes appeared to be also engaged, but he conducted me through his magnificent museum, and showed me the rarest subjects of the Animal Kingdom. The anatomical preparations were very numerous but I did not look at them, excepting to the skeletons of some quadrupeds and birds. The rooms were crowded, and I was delighted but bewildered among such a vast variety. Mr Brookes was very kind, and desired me to return on Monday, for said he, there is the choicest collection here of rare objects. Previously to my waiting upon him I had visited Hyde Park and strolled over a great part of the town. I now continued my tour and wandered on till I lost my latitude completely, and in the dusk I found myself at Westminster Abbey. At last I got to Cheapside, and then to St Pauls, and then to the Bank, and at length to my lodgings, which are near this latter place. By the way I stood with others listening a good while to the singing of a little girl on the street. I am not sure that I have ever heard a finer voice than she had - she was about ten or twelve years of age - and there was something so attracting about her that it was with difficulty that I got myself away, and not till I had given her my mite. This attraction extended to others also, for she had a little crowd about her, and several of them genteel people too. However few of them gave her anything and I was very angry at them. As I was walking along a young girl did me the honour of asking very familiarly 'Ow do ye do, my dea'. By the bye I am very partial to the English mode of speaking. In Scotland we learn the language grammatically to be sure, but we do not learn its proper pronunciation.

Sunday evening

> Crowded cities please us then
> And the busy hum of men   (Milton-L'Allegro)

True, true, but I am beginning to get tired of them. Today I crossed the Thames by London Bridge and returned by Westminster. I went through the Tower also. When I came to Westminster Abbey the doors were open and I entered. I looked at the monuments in this magnificent pile, but felt disappointed in finding the most splendid dedicated to military characters. In what respect did Major Andre and a parcel of naval captains benefit either their country or mankind so much as Watson or Paley? Yet the monument of a Lieutenant General or Rear Admiral is as splendid and as conspicuous as that of Sir Isaac Newton - and the poor poets are packed up in a corner, and one of them has 'O rare!' for an epitaph. The time will come when the glare of war will no longer dazzle our eyes. A very blockhead of a fellow who gains two or three victories more by his blunders than by his prudence is at present held higher in estimation than the man of genius and of benevolence who devotes his whole life to science and to virtue, to the improvement of his country and of mankind. It is such a man as Howard, the philanthropist, whom I would hold forth to the admiration of posterity. Yet Howard who spent his life and his fortune in the exercise of benevolence, in visiting the sick, in comforting the afflicted, in clothing the naked, in feeding the hungry, - this man who was truly formed in God's own image never had the honours bestowed on him which have been paid to a constitutionally stubborn, old blockhead who defended an English fort against a Spanish armada. 'Haugh, how that stinks!' The man who hurls most people out of the world before their time is highest in the estimation of mankind. I would have it otherwise - at least by the side of every hero I would place an eminent acoucheur! What the devil right have Alexander of Macedonia, or Frederic of Prussia to be styled Great? Alfred of England, and Peter of Russia, and Henry of France indeed have, for they had great virtues, and they advanced the prosperity of their Kingdoms. But they must all yield to John Howard and Caspar Lavater. People are all crack in the noddle, they look no farther than their noses. Things must all be changed before the world goes right. I am much mistaken if the seeds of a great revolution are not already beginning to germinate. The French revolution originated from noble principles. It is nonsense to say that its failure is a proof of its absurdity. It is one thing to conceive a plan, and another to put it in execution. Had the Prussians been three hours longer coming to the assistance of the British at Waterloo, the glory of Wellington would have perished for ever. Success is not always a proof of merit, nor is failure a proof of demerit. Before mankind acquire right views of things, there will and must be great revolutions. The sword is not sheathed, 'nation will rise against nation', and kingdoms will be divided against themselves. The necessity of reform is beginning to be seen. Divine service was performing in the Abbey and I entered the place set apart for it. I do not like the mummery of chanting and singing and reading prayers of the English Church. I hate their organs too. The noblest instrument for celebrating the praises of the Deity is that of his own formation, the human larynx. If it necessary to have another, surely the organ is not the most proper. Every note of it is so distinct, so incapable of blending, of welling, of attenuating, and so palpably composed of little harsh grating particles, I cannot bear it. It may have a different effect upon others, but no music is equal to that produced by the human voice, and from all that we know of the matter, I think I may be justified in thinking that no music is so agreeable to the Deity as it. I think too that no artificial or forced expression of praise can be equal in the sight of the Deity to a single, even momentary, heartfelt expression of gratitude. The repetition of the same form of prayer, and the number of distinct parts of which the prayer part of the service consists, are not consistent with true devotion, and I am very much inclined to think that nineteen twentieths of the congregation very devoutly say Amen to what they know nothing about. I did not see three faces in the church that had the marks of devotion in them. I observed some while bending their heads in prayer making wry faces - but I have seen worse in Scotland, for I have observed a Reverend Doctor very earnestly looking through the church to see who were in it, while at the same time addressing the deity, perhaps in these words 'Lord, may we not approach thee with our lips while our hearts are far from thee', and I have seen an old man sleeping at the communion table. The long lofty aisles of a cathedral do certainly inspire religious sentiments, but they are of a gloomy kind, and they remind me of the religion of the founders of these buildings. One half of the people in the Abbey were busy looking at the monuments during the performance of divine service, and of those who were in the place appointed for it went away as soon as the music was over. The sermon was very short, tolerable, but ill-delivered, so I came away with the crowd and spent some time looking at the monuments. I then went out and happened to stroll into the park, where a new scene presented. Dandies and whores and applemen - sober citizens, swaggering soldiers, and ragged boys, - pedestrians and equestrians, gigs, coaches, and horses. I was particularly amused with a creature having its hair curled, and its hat on one side of its head, sitting on the back of another creature whose legs were so small that a Fingalian of ordinary strength would very readily have broken them between his finger and thumb - and so languishingly delicate as the first of these animals was, and the second so spruce and frisky. The one thought he should 'witch the world with noble horsemanship' (Shakespeare), the other frisked and wheeled and capered like a kitten playing at football, or a French dancing master fencing. Everybody looked at them. I was anxious to find if it was with admiration - I could as readily perceive the expression of derision in their faces as I felt its emotion in my own mind. I wonder why people bandage their necks so straight and so stiff that before they can look behind them, they must make a full wheel. For my own part I find it more convenient to be able to look over my shoulder occasionally without moving my body. I wonder, did I say? No, I do not wonder at anything of the kind. I should rather wonder to find people acting wisely, like myself and Diogenes and Peter Pindar.

I dreamed the other night - but my candle is done and it's late.

Monday night   **'Then to the well-trode stage anon'**

I am just returned from my travels, and from Drury-lane theatre direct. But I believe it is as well to give a methodical account of transactions. And in the first place let me despatch my dream. I dreamed the other night that I was winging through the air in a large area bout three or four feet from the ground with great velocity, and I felt so very happy that I scarcely remember to have ever felt happier, and yet I have experienced happiness of no ordinary kind. The highest degree of happiness, that is of calm, tranquil, pure pleasure is that which a person feels when he is conscious of having done his duty. To my subject; the impression which this aerial tour made upon my mind was so strong that for some time after I could not prevail upon myself to believe that it did not actually happen and I can scarcely believe that it is not possible. This is an odd idea, but not quite as odd as if I were to think as some have done, that I am made of glass or bees' wax. I have dreamed such a dream before, and I must try some day if really I can skate in the air or walk across the Thames.

Today I went to the British Museum. The rooms were open at eleven, and I was among the first there. I was not surprised. I had formed high ideas of the museum of the greatest nation in the world, nor was I disappointed. It is richest in minerals and shells, but I paid most attention to the birds, particularly to the collection of British Birds which occupies a separate apartment. The system of Linnaeus has been superseded by that of Cuvier, and justly in my estimation. I was glad to find that most of my opinions regarding the genera of birds were deemed correct, for the improvements upon the Linnaean system which had occurred to me on my journey through the Western Isles last year were here realized, and I felt proud that I had been able to think for myself on such a subject, and think correctly too. However I do not altogether agree with modern ornithologists, and possibly I may become some day the author of a new system, at least I have the assurance to think so. I had promised to go and see the rest of Mr Brooke's museum today, but I could not prevail upon myself to leave the British Museum, and so I wandered through the rooms till two o'clock, and latterly began to inspect the company which came in crowds. I was amused with one creature who was acting as demonstrator to some young ladies and who was positive that a species of fish in one of the apartments was a Salamander, as he called it. I was pleased, very much pleased, to find that my opinion regarding the snake of Harris was correct, namely that it is the Anguis fragilis of Linnaeus (the slow worm), and that it is not poisonous. I felt my love of Natural History very much increased by the inspection of the museum. At the same time I felt convinced that to study nature I must have recourse to nature alone, pure and free from human interference. The division of the genus Anas (a genus of ducks), which I had proposed is here adopted - not adopted of course - but the improvement which presented itself to my mind has been anticipated, and so of several genera. Pelecanus bassanus of Linnaeus (the Gannet) is a distinct genus, as I had imagined it, and what struck me as very odd was that they had given it the very name which I had proposed to myself - Sula. I am afraid my vanity will be too much increased by this visit. At least I am now more determined to think for myself, as I have done for about two years. Ornithology is my favourite study and it will go hard with me if I do not one day merit the name of ornithologist, aye, and of Botanist too - and moreover of something else of greater importance than either. In the afternoon I went into St Paul's Cathedral. What a magnificent pile it is. It is the only thing I have seen that produces any thing like surprise. How delighted was I, on looking among the monuments, to find a statue dedicated to Howard. Yet there was a much more splendid one to the commander of a frigate who had lashed the bowsprit of a French ship to the capstan of his own, and in so doing lost his life. I was pleased also to find a statue of Johnson and another of Sir Godfrey Keller. I ascended to the top of the grand cupola, and had a glorious view of the city. A landscape of chimneys and spires stretching in all directions is certainly a very curious thing, but it is not to be compared with the majestic peaks of the Alps or Andes. In the evening I went to the theatre, where I found myself in the lower gallery among a crowd of well-dressed people. I did not like the music. It was too complicated and somehow too unnatural for my ears. I would not give one of our simple Scottish airs for all the music that Italy ever produced. What a different effect a Highland pibroch or lament would have upon me. I see the people of London have not a very fastidious taste, and that they can relish obscenity upon the stage. I did not care about the play, and came away about half past nine that I might not keep the people waiting me. Even at this time the streets were as much crowded as at mid-day. However I managed to get along at a good round trot till I got a stitch in my side, and by this time I was at St Pauls, from thence to Poultry, and then to the Bank, and then to my lodgings as usual.

London, Monday evening

I care not now to what part of the world I direct my course, not that my attachment to the scenes of my youth is rendered less firm, but that independence points out the path to other climes. Then Caledonia, I shall once more visit thee, and then a long farewell. I have today paid for a steerage passage to Aberdeen. I breakfasted with Mr Ogilvie and a German professor of languages. The marks of genius are as easily legible as those of idiocy. Mr Ogilvie is the most interesting man whom I have seen. His conversation was most edifying. I have not yet learned to express my sentiments freely before a man of abilities with whom I am not familiar but I felt highly pleased to find that many of his opinions were accordant with my own. I must not be understood as speaking of religion. I remained with Mr Ogilvie until twelve o'clock, and left him with regret. But the remembrance of his conversation produced an agreeable dream which lasted until I got to my lodging. In the afternoon I went to the wharf and took passage on one of the Aberdeen smacks, a steerage passage as I have said, for I had not money enough to get a cabin one. After this I strolled through the streets about Wapping and at length lost myself completely; and when I had ascertained my latitude I found that I had wandered nearly two miles in the wrong direction. I am not in a proper mood for writing tonight.

Old Aberdeen   Friday 12th November   8pm

My journey is now finished. I arrived here early on Saturday the 6th after a disagreeable passage of ten days from London in the smack Expert. I am again plunged into the gulf of actual existence, and I can scarcely brandish a quill. Sapient remarks and practical conclusions, and resolutions sine fine should now be made, but all these fine things I must defer till I have another journey. I have only to say that after visiting Mr Brookes and dining with Mr Ogilvie I left London on Thursday the 28th October, and after experiencing two long days of misery in the forecastle removed to the cabin, where I found good accommodation and was delighted with the conversation of an amiable young English woman, a fellow passenger.

'Vanity of vanities - all is vanity. What profit hath a man of all his labour which he taketh under the sun? For he that increaseth knowledge increaseth sorrow.

The distances travelled

From Aberdeen to Castletown of Braemar	57 miles
From Castletown to Ben-na-buird and back again	18
From Castletown to the top of Cairngorm	18
From Cairngomr to Kingussie in Badenoch	12
From Kingussie to Inverlochy	48
From Inverlochy to the top of Ben-nevis and back	8
From Inverlochy to Loch Leven ferry	13
From Loch Leven ferry to King's House	15
From King's House to Tyndrum, Perthshire	19
From Tyndrum to Cladich, Argyll	19
From Cladich to Inverary	9
From Inverary to Dunbarton	45
From Dunbarton to Glasgow	13
From Glasgow to Paisley	7
From Paisley to Irvine	21
From Irvine to Ayr	13
From Ayr to Girvan	24
From Girvan to Ballintrae	13
From Ballintrae to Portpatrick	24
From Portpatrick to Stranraer	6
From Stranraer to Newton Stewart	27
From Newton Stewart to Gatehouse	18
From Gatehouse to Castle Douglas	15
From Castle Douglas to Dumfries	19
From Dumfries to Annan	15
From Annan to Gretna	8
Length of my journey through Scotland	501 miles

From Gretna to Longtown in Cumberland	3
From Longtown to Carlisle	8
From Carlisle to Keswick	29
From Keswick to Ambleside	25
From Ambleside to Kendal	13
From Kendal to Lancaster	23
From Lancaster to Preston	22
From Preston to Manchester	32
From Manchester to Buxton, Derby-shire	24
From Buxton to Derby	34
From Derby to Leicester	26
From Leicester to Northampton	32
From Northampton to London	66
Length of my journey in England	337 miles
From Aberdeen to Gretna	501
From Gretna to London	337
	838
From London to Aberdeen by sea	about 450
	In all 1288 miles

Postscript

MacGillivray's visit to the British Museum strengthened his determination to become an ornithologist; in his own words 'to attempt an ornithology of Scotland'. There is no information on what he did for the next few years but in 1823 he was appointed to a position in Edinburgh, as assistant to Professor Robert Jameson, who held the Regius Chair of Natural History at the University there. He had one of the biggest collections of natural history specimens in Britain and MacGillivray was responsible for its care. In 1831 he was appointed as Conservator of the Museum of the Royal College of Surgeons in Edinburgh and remained in the post for ten years, a decade which was very productive for him. He published books on botany, geology, on scientific biography, and the first three volumes of his major work, a History of British Birds. In 1830 he met the American bird artist John James Audubon, the famous American bird artist. The two men became life-long friends and between laid the foundation for ornithology in their respective countries, MacGillivray with his History of British Birds and Audubon with The Birds of America and the accompanying letter press, the Ornithological Biographies, which was largely written by MacGillivray.

In 1841 MacGillivray returned to his native city, as the Regius Professor of Natural History at Marischal College, a remarkable achievement, considering his humble beginnings. He was a well-loved teacher, but he also carried on writing and publishing, his final achievement being the fifth and last volume of the History of British Birds published a few weeks before his death in 1852.

MacGillivray has never received the credit that his scientific achievements merited. He made enemies carelessly and easily, enemies in the scientific establishment of the day who, by critical reviews, prevented a wide appreciation of the worth of his books. He developed his own unorthodox scheme of bird classification, a scheme which was flawed and never gained favour, but he also lived in a time of growing interest in science, and more popular, more accessible, and scientifically less worthy works on British ornithology came to overshadow his own.

He remains Scotland's greatest field naturalist, an unrivalled recorder of the natural world and one of Britain's finest ornithologists.

APPENDIX

In several places in his journal MacGillivray recorded the plants that he had seen during a particular day or when travelling across a particular piece of countryside. These lists represents prodigious feats of memory; he listed the plants seen during the different parts of the walk, and the plants seen in and out of flower. In his list MacGillivray recorded the plants using their Latin names. I have followed this but have also added their common English names; I have used the names that MacGillivray would have used for them, taking them from the 6th edition of MacGillivray's revised version of Withering's *A Systematic Arrangment of British Plants*. This was a very successful book that appeared in 13 editions between 1830 and 1860. Most of the common names are the same as today's familiar names.

The plants seen between Aberdeen and Charlestown of Aboyne

Between Blacks Brewery, or the mouth of the river and the bridge, a distance of upwards of a mile I observed the following plants; those in flower

Senecio jacobea Common Ragwort
Apargia autumnalis Autumnal Hawk-bit
Senecio vulgaris Common Groundsel
Achillea Millefolium Common Yarrow
Hypochaeris radicata Long-rooted Cat's-ear
Sinapis arvensis Field Mustard
Sonchus arvensis Corn Sow-thistle
Polygonum aviculare Common Knot-grass
Centaurea nigra Black Knapweed
Chaerophyllum sylvestre Cow-parsley
Ranunculus acris Upright Meadow Crowfoot
Thlaspi bursa-pastoris Common Shepherd's-purse
Galium verum Common Yellow Bed-straw
Alisma plantago Great Water Plantain
Valeriana officinalis Great Wild Valerian
Campanula rotundifolia Common Bell-flower

Scabiosa succisa Devil's-bit Scabious
Matricaria chamomilla Common Wild Chamomile

those out of flower
Spiraea ulmaria Meadow-sweet
Potamogeton natans Broad-leaved Pond-weed
Ulex Europaeus Gorse
Pteris aquilina Common Brake
Equisetum Horse-tail
Veronica beccabunga Short-leaved Water Speedwell
Juncus effusus Soft Rush
Juncus acutiflorus Sharp-flowered Rush
Sparganium ramosum Branched Bur-reed
Rumex obtusifolius Broad-leaved Dock
Urtica dioica Great Nettle

The plants observed between the Bridge of Dee and Upper Banchory are the following; plants in flower

Senecio Jacobaea Common Ragwort
Erica vulgaris Common Ling
Angelica sylvestris Wild Angelica
Campanula rotundifolia Common Bell-flower
Prunella vulgaris Self-heal
Ranunculus hederaceus Ivy-leaved Crowfoot
Centaurea nigra Black Knapweed
Alchemilla vulgaris Common Lady's mantle
Myosotis palustris Great Water Scorpion Grass
Galium verum Common Yellow Bed-straw
Lapsana communis Common Nipple-wort
Epilobium sp Willow-herb
Achillea Millefolium Common Yarrow
Stellaria graminea Lesser Stitchwort
Senecio sylvaticus Mountain Groundsel

Valeriana officianalis Great Wild Valerian
Rubus fruticosus Common Bramble
Erica cinerea Common Heath
Senecio aquaticus Marsh Ragwort
Chrysanthemum segetum Corn Marigold
Mentha hirsuta Hairy Mint
Sinapis arvensis Field Mustard
Vicia cracca Tufted Vetch
Ranunculus flammula Less Spear-wort
Matricaria chamomilla Common Wild Chamomile
Hypochoris radicata Long-rooted Cat's-ear
Thymus serpyllum Wild Thyme
Senecio viscosus Stinking Groundsel
Trifolium repens White Trefoil
Tormentilla officianalis Common Tormentil Septfoil
Cnicus lanceolatus Spear Thistle
Thlaspi bursa-pastoris Common Shepherd's-purse
Euphrasia officinalis Eye-bright
Galeopsis tetrahit Common Hemp-nettle
Erica tetralix Cross-leaved Heath
Teesdalia nudicaulis Naked-stalked Teesdalia
Urtica urens Small Nettle
Digitalis purpurea Foxglove
Linum catharticum Purging Flax
Polygonum aviculare Common Knot-grass
Polygonum persicaria Spotted Persicaria
Stachys arvensis Corn Woundwort
Pimpinella saxifraga Common Burnet-saxifrage
Viola tricolor Pansy Violet
Bellis perennis Common Daisy
Scabiosa succisa Devil's-bit Scabious
Geranium molle Common Dove's-foot Crane's-bill
Apargia autumnalis Autumnal Hawkbit
Plantago lanceolatus Ribwort Plaintain

Veronica serpyllifolia Smooth Speedwell
Veronica officianalis Common Speedwell
Hieracium prenanthoides Rough-bordered Hawkweed
Alchemilla arvensis Parsley Piert
Myrica gale Sweet Gale
Viola canina Dog"s Violet
Orobus tuberosus Heath-pea
Reseda luteola Wild Woad

Plants out of flower
Cnicus arvensis Field Thistle
Raphanus raphanistrum Field Radish
Spiraea ulmaria Meadow-sweet
Ranunculus acris Upright Meadow Crowfoot
Polygonum convolvulus Black Bindweed
Sonchus arvensis Corn Sow-thistle
Euphorbia helioscopia Sun Spurge
Juncus effusus Soft Rush
Cnicus palustris Marsh Thistle
Geranium robertianum Herb Robert
Urtica dioica Great Nettle
Lotus major Greater Bird's-foot Trefoil
Stachys sylvatica Hedge Woundwort
Rumex obtusifolius Broad-leaved Dock
Achillea ptarmica Sneeze-wort
Chaerophyllum sylvestre Cow-parsley
Conium maculatum Common Hemlock
Juncus conglomeratus Common Rush
Scrophularia nodosa Knotted-rooted Figwort
Ranunculus repens Creeping Crowfoot
Rubus idaeus Raspberry Bush
Juncus acutifloris Sharp-flowered Rush
Cerastium viscosum Narrow-leaved Mouse-eared Chickweed
Plantago lanceolata Ribwort Plantain

Triticum repens Creeping Wheat-grass
Scleranthus annuus Annual Knawel
Lolium perenne Common Rye-grass
Galium saxatile Smooth Heath Bed-straw
Rumex crispus Curled Dock
Bromus mollis Soft Brome-grass
Juncus squarrosus Moss Rush
Scandix odorata Sweet Cicely
Plantago media Hoary Plantain
Plantago maritima Sea Plantain
Holcus lanatus Meadow Soft-grass
Geum urbanum Common Avens
Aira caryophyllea Silver Hair-grass
Holcus avenaceus Oat-like Soft-grass
Veronica chamadrys Germander Speedwell
Nardus stricta Mat-grass
Rumex acetosa Common Sorrel
Galium aparine Goose-grass
Arenaria rubra Purple Sandwort
Tenacetum vulgare Common Tansy
Artemesia vulgaris Mugwort
Cerastium vulgatum Broad-leaved Mouse-eared Chick-weed
Ulex europaeus Gorse
Chenopodium album White Goose-foot
Vicia sepium Common Bush Vetch
Spergula arvensis Corn Spurrey
Stellaria uliginosa Bog Stitchwort
Juniperis communis Common Juniper
Gnaphalium uliginosum Marsh Cudweed
Hypericum humifusum Trailing St. John's-wort
Fragaria vesca Wood Strawberry
Rosa villosa Soft-leaved Round-fruited Rose
Vaccinium myrtillus Bilberry
Solidago virgaurea Common Golden-rod

Rumex acetosella Sheep's Sorrel
Tussilago farfara Colt's-foot
Rosa canina Common Dog Rose
Lotus corniculatus Common Bird's-foot Trefoil

The ferns seen in this course were
Pteris aquilina Common Brake
Equisetum arvensis Corn Horse-tail
Polypodium vulgare Common Polypody
Aspidium felix-mas Male Shield-fern
Aspidium felix-fomina Female Shield-fern
Equisetum sylvaticum Wood Horse-tail
Blechnum boreale Northern Hard-fern

The plants seen between Upper Banchory and Charlestown of Aboyne are the following; out of flower

Scabiosa succisa Devil's-bit Scabious
Galium verum Common Yellow Bedstraw
Erica cinerea Common Heath
Erica vulgaris Common Ling
Tormentilla officinalis Common Tormentil Septfoil
Euphraisa officinalis Eye-bright
Ranunculus flammula Less Spearwort
Pedicularis sylvatica Common Lousewort
Bellis perennis Common Daisy
Senecio jacobaea Common Ragwort
Apargia autumnalis Autumnal Hawkbit
Lotus corniculatus Common Bird's-foot Trefoil
Erica tetralix Cross-leaved Heath
Campanula rotundifolia Round-leaved Bell-flower
Carduus palustris Marsh Thistle
Hypochaeris radicata Long-rooted Cat's-ear
Polygonum persicaria Spotted Persicaria

Pimpinella saxifraga Common Burnet-saxifrage
Achillea ptarmica Sneeze-wort
Cerastium viscosum Narrow-leaved Mouse-eared Chickweed
Linum catharticum Purging Flax
Cnicus arvensis Field Thistle
Ranunculus acris Upright Meadow Crowfoot
Statice armeria Common Thrift
Stachys arvensis Corn Woundwort
Matricaria chamomilla Common Wild Chamomile
Mentha hirsuta Hairy Mint
Centaurea nigra Black Knapweed
Viola tricolor Pansy Violet
Thlaspi bursa-pastoris Common Shepherd's Purse
Euphorbia helioscopia Sun Spurge
Trifolium pratense Common Purple Clover
Polygonum aviculare Common Knot-grass
Chrysanthemum segmentum Corn Marigold
Scleranthus annuus Annual Knawel
Radiola millegrana All-seed
Galeopsis versicolor Large-flowered Hemp-nettle
Senecio aquaticus Marsh Ragwort
Galeopsis tetrahit Common Hemp-nettle
Achillea millefolium Common Yarrow
Spergula nodosa Knotted Spurre
Myosotis arvensis Common Field Scorpion-grass
Thymus serpyllum Wild Thyme
Parnassia palustris Common Grass of Parnassus
Centaurea cyanus Corn Blue-bottle
Cnicus lanceolatus Spear Thistle
Senecio vulgaris Common Groundsel
Trifolium repens White Trefoil
Hieracium pilosella Mouse-Hawkweed
Leontodon taraxacum Common Dandelion

Plants out of flower (written at 8 AM the next morning)

Aira caespitosa Turfy Hair-grass
Cnicus lanceolatus Spear Thistle
Thymus serpyllum Wild Thyme
Veronica officinalis Common Speedwell
Prunus spinosa Blackthorn
Teucrium scorodoniu Wood Sage
Juniperis communis Common Juniper
Ranunculus repens Creeping Crowfoot
Rumex acetosella Sheep's Sorrel
Sonchus oleracus Common Sow-thistle
Hypericum pulchrum Small Upright St. John's Wort
Juncus conglomeratus Common Rush
Chenopodium album White Goose-foot
Tussilago farfara Colt's-foot
Spiraea ulmaria Meadow-sweet
Myrica gale Sweet Gale
Rosa villosa Soft-leaved Round-fruited Rose
Leontodon taraxacum Common Dandelion
Vaccinium myrtillus Bilberry
Rubus idaeus Raspberry Bush
Angelica sylvestris Wild Angelica
Lonicera periclymenum Common Honeysuckle
Rubus fruticosus Common Bramble
Veronica chamaedrys Germander Speedwell
Potamogeton heterophyllus Various-leaved Pond-weed
Ulex europaeus Common Gorse
Prunella vulgaris Self-heal
Plantago media Hoary Plaintain
Rumex acetosella Sheep's Sorrel
Rumex obtusifolius Broad-leaved Dock
Potamageton natans Broad-leaved Pond-weed
Aira caryophyllea Silver Hair-grass

Stellaria media Common Chickweed
Myriophyllum spicatum Spiked Water-milfoil
Holcus avenaceus Oat-like Soft-grass
Menyanthes trifoliata Marsh Trefoi
Juncus effusus Soft Rush
Spergula arvensis Corn Spurrey
Rosa canina Dog Rose
Juncus acutiflorus Sharp-flowered Rush
Viola canina Dog's Violet
Arbutus uva-ursi Red Bear-berry
Pyrola rotundifolia Round-leaved Winter-green
Triglochin palustre Marsh Arrow-grass
Veronica officinalis Common Speedwell
Narthecium ossifragum Bog Ashphodel
Nardus stricta Mat-grass
Pedicularis sylvatica Common Lousewort
Rhinanthus crista-galli Yellow Rattle
Fragaria vesca Wood Strawberry
Aira praecox Early Hair-grass
Anthoxanthum odoratum Sweet-scented Spring-grass
Solidago virgaurea Common Golden-rod
Hydrocotyle vulgaris Marsh Penny
Veronica serpyllifolia Smooth Speedwell
Alchemilla vulgaris Common Lady's Mantle
Comarum palustre Marsh Cinquefoil
Gnaphalium dioicum Mountain Cudweed
Galium palustre White Water Bed-straw
Geranium robertianum Herb Robert
Montia fontana Water Chickweed
Anthyllis vulneraria Kidney-vetch
Caltha palustris Common Marsh Marigold
Gnaphalium uliginosum Marsh Cudweed
Silene maritima Sea Campion
Pinguicula vulgaris Common Butterwort

Eriophorum angustifolium Common Cotton-grass
Alchemilla alpina Alpine Lady's Mantle
Scirpus lacustris Bull-rush
Gentiana campestris Field Gentian
Pedicularis palustris Marsh Lousewort

Ferns
Pteris aquilina Common Brake
Equisetum arvensis Corn Horse-tail
Aspidium felix-mas Male Shield-fern
Aspidium felix-fomina Female Shield-fern
Equisetum sylvaticum Wood Horse-tail
Blechnum boreale Northern Hard-fern
Lycopodium clavatum Common Club-moss

The plants seen between Charlestown of Aboyne and Castletown of Braemar
Those seen between Charlestown of Aboyne and the Pass of Ballater; those in flower

Erica vulgaris Common Ling
Achillea millefolium Common Yarrow
Saxifraga azoides Yellow Mountain Saxifrage
Campanula rotundifera Common Bell-flower
Tormentilla officinalis Common Tormentil Septfoil
Ranunculus flammula Lesser Spearwort
Erica cinerea Common Heath
Linum catharticum Purging Flax
Scabiosa succisa Devil's-bit Scabious
Galium verum Common Yellow Bedstraw
Erica tetralix Cross-leaved Heath
Polygala vulgaris Common Milkwort
Apargia autumnalis Autumnal Hawkbit
Lotus corniculatus Common Bird's-foot Trefoil

those out of flower

Thymus serpyllum Wild Thyme

Veronica officinalis Common Speedwell

Veronica chamadrys Germander Speedwell

Aspidium felix-mas Male Shield-fern

Galium uluginosum Rough Marsh Bed-straw

Gnaphalium dioicum Mountain Cud-weed

Pteris aquilina   Common Brake

Lycopodium clavatum Common Club-moss

Juniperis communis Common Juniper

Aria praecox Early Hair-grass

Gentiana campestris Field Gentian

Prunella vulgaris Self-heal

Orobus tuberosus Heath Pea

Bellis perennis Common Daisy

Myrica gale Sweet Gale

Hypericum pulchrum Small Upright St. John's Wort

Lycopodium selaginoides Prickly Club-moss

Juncus squarrosus Moss Rush

Rosa canina Dog Rose

Veronica beccabunga Short-leaved Water Speedwell

Teucrium scorodonia Wood Sage

Rosa villosa Soft-leaved Round-fruited Rose

Genista angelica Needle Green-weed

Arbutus uva-ursi Red Bear-berry

Rosa spinosissima Burnet Rose

I also saw Scrophularia nodosa Needle-rooted Figwort and Tenacetum vulgare Common Tansy, but in a cultivated place.

The plants seen while climbing Ben Nevis from Fort William Those seen in Glen Nevis.

Scabiosa succisa Devil's-bit Scabious

Plantago lanceolata Ribwort Plaintain

Euphrasia officinalis Eyebright
Centaurea nigra Black Knapweed
Tormentilla officinalis Common Tormentil Septfoil
Galium saxatile Smooth Heath Bed-straw
Cynosurus cristatus Crested Dog's-tail-grass
Trifolium pratense Common Purple Clover
Aspidium felix-mas Male Shield-fern
Rumex obtusifolius Broad-leaved Dock
Geranium sylvaticum Wood Crane's-bill
Erica vulgaris Common Ling
Achillea millefolium Common Yarrow
Rumex acetosa Common Sorrel
Apargia autumnalis Autumnal Hawkbit
Achillea ptarmica Sneeze-wort
Mercurialis perennis Perennial Mercury
Cnicus lanceolatus Spear Thistle
Stachys palustris Marsh Woundwort
Veronica chamadrys Germander Speedwell
Pedicularis sylvatica Common Lousewort
Vicia sepium Common Bush Vetch
Juncus effusus Soft Rush
Plantago maritima Sea Plaintain
Prunella vulgaris Self-heal
Holcus avenaceus Oat-like Soft-grass
Juncus squarrosus Moss Rush
Polygonum persicaria Spotted Persicaria
Plantago media Hoary Plantain
Ranunculus flammula Lesser Spear-wort
Ranunculus repens Creeping Crowfoot
Galeopsis tetrahit Common Hemp-nettle
Rhinathus crista-galli Yellow Rattle
Pimpinella saxifraga Common Burnet-saxifrage
Spergula arvensis Corn Spurrey
Lotus corniculatus Common Bird's-foot Trefoil

Hypochaeris radicata Long-rooted Cat's-ear
Sinapsis arvensis Field Mustard
Nardus stricta Mat-grass
Spiraea ulmaria Meadow Sweet
Ranunculus acris Upright Meadow Crowfoot
Pteris aquilina Common Brake
Solidago virgaurea Common Golde-rod
Cerastium viscosum Narrow-leaved Mouse-eared Chickweed
Oxalis acetosella Common Wood-sorrel
Chaerophyllum sylvestre Cow-parsley
Hieracium prenanthoides Rough-bordered Hawkweed
Holcus lanatus Meadow Soft-grass

The trees were Common Alder, Common Ash, and Scotch Fir, which appeared to be planted.

The plants seen at the base of the mountain to nearly one third of the way up were;
Betula alba White Birch
Coryllus avellana Common Hazel
Erica vulgaris Common Ling
Mespilus oxycantha Hawthorn
Vaccinium myrtillus Bilberry
Pteris aquilina Common Brake
Apargia autumnalis Autumnal Hawkbit
Fragaria vesca Wood Strawberry
Narthecium ossifragum Bog Asphodel
Prunella vulgaris Self-heal
Trifolium repens White Trefoil
Tormentilla officinalis Common Tormentil Septfoil
Scabiosa succisa Devil's-bit Scabious
Rhinanthus crista-galli Yellow Rattle
Pedicularis sylvatica Common Lousewort
Erica cinerea Common Heath

Euphrasia officinalis Eyebright
Parnassia palustris Common Grass of Parnassus
Juncus effusus Soft Rush
Pinguicula vulgaris Common Butterwort
Ranunculus acris Upright meadow Crowfoot
Spiraea ulmaria Meadow-sweet
Viola canina Dog's Violet
Polygala vulgaris Common Milkwort
Digitalis purpurea Common Fox-glove
Hypericum pulchrum Small Upright St. John's Wort
Rumex acetosa Common Sorrel
Veronica officinalis Common Speedwell
Solidago virgaurea Common Golden-rod
Galium saxatile Smooth Heath Bed-straw
Rubus saxatilis Stone Bramble
Linum catharticum Purging Flax
Trifolium pratense Common Purple Clover

From the termination of this division, above which no trees grew, to the commencement of the stony and sterile part, the plants seen were;
Erica vulgaris Common Ling
Vaccinium myrtillus Bilberry
Prunella vulgaris Self-heal
Tormentilla officinalis Common Tormentil Septfoil
Rhinanthus crista-galli Yellow Rattle
Erica cinerea Common Heath
Euphrasia officinalis Eyebright
Parnassia palustris Common Grass of Parnassus
Pinguicula vulgaris Common Butterwort
Viola canina Dog's Violet
Polygala vulgaris Common Milkwort
Galium saxatile Smooth Heath Bed-straw
Rubus saxatilis Stone Bramble
Linum catharticum Purging Flax

Trifolium pratense Common Purple Clover
Rumex acetosa Common Sorrel
Chryosplenium oppositifolium Opposite-leaved Golden-saxifrage
Arbutus uva-ursi Red Bear-berry
Lycopodium selaginoides Prickly Club-moss
Oxalis acetosella Common Wood-sorrel
Blechnum boreale Northern Hard-fern
Lycopodium clavatum Common Club-moss
Thymus serpyllum Wild Thyme
Empetrum nigrum Common Crow-berry
Anthoxanthum odoratum Sweet-scented Spring-grass
Saxifraga aizoides Yellow Mountain Saxifrage
Saxifraga stellaris Starry Saxifrage
Spiraea ulmaria Meadow-sweet
Lycopodium selago Fir Club-moss
Lycopodium alpinum Savin-leaved Club-moss
Alchemilla alpina Alpine Lady's Mantle
Sagina procumbens Procumbent Pearl-wort
Epilobium alpinum Alpine Willow-herb

The plants seen in the region of sterility were;
Silene maritima Sea Campion
Pteris crispa Curled Brake
Lycopodium alpinum Savin-leaved Club-moss
Saxifraga stellaris Starry Saxifrage
Alchemilla alpina Alpine Lady's Mantle
Gnaphalium supinum Dwarf Alpine Cudweed

This is very far from being a complete list of the plants growing on Ben-nevis. It serves only to show what sort of plants grow upon it. The accuracy of the list may be depended upon.

The plants seen between Fort William and King's House, Argyllshire. Trees and shrubs

Alnus glutinosa Quercus robur Common Oak
Prunus spinosa Blackthorn
Rubus fructicosus Common Bramble
Corylus avellana Common Hazel
Mespilus oxycantha Hawthorn
Lonicera peryclymenun Common Honeysuckle
Rubus idaesus Raspberry Bush
Erica vulgaris Common Ling
Hedera helix Common Ivy
Fraxinus excelsior Common Ash
Erica cinerea Common Heath
Betula alba White Birch
Hypericum androsomum Tutsan
Erica tetralix Cross-leaved Heath
Pyrus aucuparia Mountain Ash
Myrica gale Sweet Gale
Rosa canina Common Dog Rose

The ferns were;
Pteris aquilina Common Brake
Aspidium felix-mas Male Shield-fern
Aspidium felix-fomina Female Shield-fern
Blechnum boreale Northern Hard-fern
Polypodium vulgare Common Polypody
Asplenium ruta-muraria Wall-rue Spleenwort

The plants which occurred in cultivated ground were;
Spergula arvensis Corn Spurrey
Polygonum persicaria Spotted Persicaria
Myosotis arvensis Common Field Scorpion-grass
Stachys palustris Marsh Woundwort
Senecio vulgaris Common Groundsel
Galeopsis versicolor Large Flowered hemp-nettle
Holcus avenaceus Oat-like Soft-grass

Vicia sepium Common Bush Vetch
Polygonum convolvulus Black Bindweed
Triticum repens Creeping Wheat-grass

The other plants seen, each in its peculiar soil or situation, are;
Parnassia palustris Common Grass of Parnassus
Linum catharticum Purging Flax
Senecio aquaticus Marsh Ragwort
Apargia autumnalis Autumnal Hawkbit
Solidago virgaurea Comon Golden-rod
Lysimachia nemorum Wood Loose-strife
Lolium perenne Common Rye-grass
Pinguicula vulgaris Common Butterwort
Aira caespitosa Turfy Hair-grass
Artemisia vulgaris Mugwort
Hypericum pulchrum Small Upright St. John's-wort
Cynosurus cristatus Crested Dog's-tail-grass
Polygonum amphibium Amphibious Persicaria
Epilobium montanum Broad Smooth-leaved Willow-herb
Agrostis vulgaris Fine Bent-grass
Potentilla anserina Goose-grass
Viola canina Dog's Violet
Saxifraga azoides Yellow Mountain Saxifrage
Rumex obtusifolius Broad-leaved Dock
Geranium robertianum Herb Robert
Dactylis glomerata Cock's-foot-grass
Rumex acetosa Common Sorrel
Cnicus palustris Marsh Thistle
Bellis perennis Common Daisy
Plantago media Hoary Plaintain
Plantago lanceolata Ribwort Plaintain
Gentiana campestris Field Gentian
Urtica dioica Great Nettle
Melica caerulea Purple Melic-grass

Sagina procumbens Procumbent Pearl-wort
Trifolium repens White Trefoil
Pedicularis sylvatica Common Lousewort
Chyrsanthemum segetum Corn Marigold
Trifolium pratense Common Purple Clover
Ranunculus flammula Lesser Spearwort
Ranunculus repens Creeping Crowfoot
Campanula rotundiflora Common Bell-flower
Centaurea nigra Black Knapweed
Polygala vulgaris Common Milkwort
Chaerophyllum sylvestre Cow-parsley
Juncus squarrosus Moss Rush
Matricaria chamomilla Common Wild Chamomile
Cnicus lanceolatus Spear Thistle
Menyanthes trifoliata Marsh Trefoil
Scabiosa succissa Devil's-bit Scabious
Oxalis acetosella Common Wood-sorrel
Viola palustris Marsh Violet
Juncus acutifloris Sharp-flowered Rush
Mercurialis perennis Perennial Mercury
Vaccinum myrtillus Bilberry
Rhinanthus crista-galli Yellow-rattle
Senecio jacobaea Common Ragwort
Veronica officinalis Common Speedwell
Spiraea ulmaria Meadow-sweet
Triglochin palustre Marsh Arrow-grass
Lotus corniculatus Common Bird's-foot Trefoil
Achillea millefolium Common Yarrow
Plantago maritima Sea Plantain
Polygonum hydropiper Biting Persicaria
Juncus conglomeratus Common Rush
Arctium lappa Burdock
Holcus lanatus Meadow Soft-grass
Angelica sylvestris Wild Angelica

Ranunculus acris Upright Meadow Crowfoot
Prunella vulgaris Self Heal
Pedicularis palustris Marsh Lousewort
Sonchus oleracus Common Sow-thistle
Galium saxatile Smooth Heath Bed-straw
Iris pseudacorus Yellow-iris
Bromus mollis Soft Bromw-grass
Narthecium ossifragum Bog Asphodel
Veronica chamaedrys Germander Speedwell
Lathyrus pratensis Yellow Meadow Vetchling
Juncus effusus Soft Rush
Hieracium prenanthoides Rough-bordered Hawkweed
Stachys sylvatica Hedge Woundwort
Digitalis purpurea Common Fox-glove
Lapsana communis Common Nipple-wort
Valeriana officinalis Great Wild Valerian
Teucrium scorodina Wood Sage
Fragaria vesca Wood Strawberry
Scrophularia nodosa Knotted-rooted Figwort
Euphrasia officinalis Eyebright
Caltha palustris Common Marsh Marigold
Circaea alpina Mountain Enchanter's Nightshade
Tormentilla officinalis Common Tormentil Septfoil
Geranium dissectum Jagged-leaved Crane's-bill
Cnicus arvensis Field Thistle
Sedum anglicum White English Stonecrop
Thymus serpyllum Wild Thyme
Myosotis palustris Great Water Scorpion-grass
Atriplex patula Spreading Halbert-shaped   Orache (on the seashore)